THE
LANGUAGE
OF LONDON

THE
LANGUAGE
OF LONDON

COCKNEY RHYMING SLANG

Daniel Smith

Michael O'Mara Books Limited

First published in Great Britain in 2011 by
Michael O'Mara Books Limited
9 Lion Yard
Tremadoc Road
London SW4 7NQ

A CIP catalogue record for this book is available from the British Library.

Papers used by Michael O'Mara Books Limited are natural, recyclable products made from wood grown in sustainable forests. The manufacturing processes conform to the environmental regulations of the country of origin.

ISBN: 978-1-84317-574-2

1 2 3 4 5 6 7 8 9 10

www.mombooks.com

Cover design by Ana Bjezancevic

Designed and typeset by K DESIGN, Winscombe, Somerset

Printed and bound in Great Britain by Clays Ltd, St Ives plc

FOR ROSIE,
THE TROUBLE AND STRIFE

CONTENTS

Introduction   9

Someone to Rabbit and Pork To: Family Life   13

China Plates: Friends   18

Gates of Rome: Home   24

Tooting and Tiddlywink: Food and Drink   33

Lord Mayoring: Swearing, Insults and Banter   43

Night and Day: Play and Leisure   50

Rub-a-dub: The Pub   55

A Day at the Belt and Braces: Sport and Gambling   64

Harold Macmillans: A Life of Crime   72

Smile and Smirk: The World of Work   82

Tate and Lyle: Style and Apparel   91

Big Ears and Noddy: Body   99

Visiting My Aunt's: Bodily Functions   111

Shillings and Pence: The Mind and the Senses   116

Tom and Dick: Health   124

Oedipus Rex: Sex   130

Harry Lime, Drum and Bass, Hat and Feather:
    Time, Place and Weather   135

The Frog and Toad: Transport and Travel   144

Adam and Eve: Religion   149

English to Slang Index   153

INTRODUCTION

Slang comes in many different forms but they are all essentially informal 'secret languages', in which particular words are replaced with other words and phrases to hide the meaning of a sentence from those not versed in that particular slang code.

If you asked a sample of people to name a particular sort of slang, you could almost guarantee that Cockney rhyming slang would be the most common answer. The *Oxford English Dictionary* defines rhyming slang thus: 'a variety of (orig. Cockney) slang in which a word is replaced by a phrase which rhymes with it'. The pattern is, by and large, straightforward: take your subject word and replace it with a short phrase (typically two or three words), in which the last word rhymes with the subject word. Then contract the phrase so that the rhyming word is left out (a process that according to Bill Bryson goes under the technical name 'hemiteleia'), leaving you with a code designed to mystify those whose ears are not attuned. The general pattern in neatly demonstrated in this example of perhaps the best known of all rhyming slang phrases:

stairs (subject word) ® *apples and pears* (rhyming phrase)
® *apples* (how the phrase is commonly rendered)

Rhyming slang is always changing and evolving, unconstrained by formal rules. Indeed, even to think of it as a distinctly Cockney language is outdated. While it emerged on the streets of London, it is now used by a community that lives far outside those narrow boundaries. In its early days it was the language of costermongers (street traders) and criminals who did not want word of their business to fall on the wrong ears. But there were all sorts of other influences too. London had long been a destination for immigrants and many of these groups brought with them distinct slangs of their own, notably the Jewish population, the Irish, the Huguenots and the Romanies. The docks, a melting pot of international cultures, birthed yet more slang forms, as did London's theatre community. Each group contributed to the rich slang culture that thrived in the capital.

When Cockney rhyming slang first appeared on the scene is a contentious question but it is fair to say that it was widespread by the mid-nineteenth century and reached a peak of popularity in the early part of the twentieth century (perhaps as a result of the fluid social contacts that occurred as a result of the First World War). John Camden Hotten is generally credited with being the first person to talk specifically of Cockney rhyming slang, in his 1859 *Dictionary of Modern Slang, Cant and Vulgar Words*. He suggested its roots lay in the 1840s, though he 'credits' the criminal classes rather than the street traders:

The cant, which has nothing to do with that spoken by the costermongers, is known in Seven Dials and elsewhere as the Rhyming Slang, or the substitution of words and sentences which rhyme with other words intended to be kept secret. I learn that the rhyming slang was introduced about twelve or fifteen years ago.

Around the same time that Hotten published his study, a certain Duncange Anglicus was writing *The Vulgar Tongue: A Glossary of Slang, Cant, and Flash Words and Phrases used in London*. A review of it appeared in the *Athenaeum*, a popular literary magazine of the day, in January 1859 and hints at the rapidly growing popularity of the city's informal idioms:

Now that Slang is everywhere fashionable,—in the street, on the platform, in the drawing-room—this curious little handbook of 'The Vulgar Tongue' cannot fail of success. Our fair readers who wish to captivate our bold sex may here find the prettiest phrases, and our country cousins who would perfect themselves in 'the flash words principally used in London,' as now and then made public through the medium of those very interesting police reports, cannot do better than 'nab the chance,' and buy this 'leary little book.'

However, not everybody was in favour of its spread. In Carlisle the Revd A. Mursell delivered a sermon full of concern that 'there are many young men who seem to consider it essential to manliness that they should be masters of slang . . . It comes with its hordes of barbarous words, threatening the entire extinction of genuine English.' He grossly overstated the case, but there was a grain of truth in what he said for several of the phrases from those earliest days – *apples and pears* for *stairs* and *mince pies* for *eyes* among them – remain in use to this day.

Inspirations for rhyming slang phrases comes from all sorts of sources. You will see examples, for instance, from the geography of London itself, the music hall, sports, nursery rhymes, literature (especially Charles Dickens) and, particularly in the case of more modern additions, the world of celebrity.

While you'll probably struggle to hear it spoken on every major London street as you might have done in times gone by, rhyming slang remains very much alive, not least through its regular depictions on TV and in films. From musicals like *Me and My Girl* and *Fings Ain't What They Used T'Be* to classic shows such as *Till Death Us Do Part*, *Minder*, *Only Fools and Horses*, *Porridge*, *The Sweeney* and *EastEnders*, new generations are introduced to its subtleties.

Be warned though, this is a language born of the streets and as such it pulls few punches. At times clever, informed and amusing, it can also be rude enough to make a sailor blush. But above all, rhyming slang for the modern user should be fun. So make yourself a dog of rosy, take the weight off your plates and cast your minces over the pages of this rookery.

SOMEONE TO RABBIT AND PORK TO: FAMILY LIFE

Rabbit and pork – *Talk* (relying on a Cockney pronunciation of 'talk' as 'tawk' and 'pork' as 'pawk'). This slang item was immortalized in a song by Chas and Dave in which the speaker considers getting rid of his otherwise perfect girl on the basis that 'No, you won't stop talkin', / why dont you give it a rest?' Her utterances were memorably summarized thus: 'Yup yup rabbit yup yup yup rabbit rabbit bunny jabber yup rabbit bunny yup yup.'

—∞—

However much the average Cockney rhymer might claim to be tired of being nagged, they never forget that family always come first. So while some of the slang in this section might be gently mocking, it is always ultimately affectionate.

* **Baker's dozen** – *cousin*. A baker's dozen is, of course, thirteen, since in the thirteenth century the punishments that a baker could be subjected to if found guilty of cheating his customers (which included the hacking off of a hand) ensured that they over-supplied on their orders.

13

* **Basin of gravy** – *baby*. One of rhyming slang's least convincing rhymes!

* **Bottle of porter** – *daughter*. Porter is a stout-like beer made from dark malts, supposedly named for its popularity in the eighteenth century with the many porters who worked the streets and waterways of London. Its use here might allude to the fatherly 'wetting of the baby's head'.

* **Cow and kisses** – *missus* (as in 'the wife'). A mid-Victorian rhyme and sometimes suggested as responsible for the usage of 'cow' for an objectionable woman.

* **Currant bun** – *son*.

* **Gawd forbid** – *kid*. An exclamation suggestive of some sort of failing in family planning procedures. *Saucepan lid* is sometimes used as an alternative.

* **God love her** – *mother*. At least until they are married, the most important figure in any Cockney's life is their old mum, and this rhyme reflects the high esteem in which she is held. However, out of the matriarch's hearing, the rather more suggestive phrase *strangle and smother* is also used.

* **Jack Sprat** – *brat*. A reference to the subject of the English nursery rhyme who followed a non-fat diet and had a plump wife.

* **Jam tart** – *sweetheart*. A rhyme redolent of gooiness and comfort.

* **Light of my life** – *wife*. The slang used by a husband in front of his better half. But in much commoner currency is *trouble and strife*, usually muttered with an archly raised eyebrow. A further rhyme is *Duchess of Fife*, dating from the nineteenth century. The 1st Duchess was Louise, the Princess Royal (daughter of Edward VII and sister of George V). The rhyme is usually contracted to Dutch (e.g. 'my old dutch') although its rhyming origins have been largely forgotten.

* **Manhole cover** – *brother*. An unlikely rhyme that does, however, emphasize the masculine gender.

* **Mother of Pearl** – *old girl*. Used in general for a wife of many years' standing.

* **Mother's pride** – *bride*. A rhyme that speaks of happiness and celebration. Its alternative is the rather less becoming *fat and wide*, derived from the juvenile reworking of Richard Wagner's 'Bridal Chorus' with the lyrics 'Here comes the bride, all fat and wide / See how she wobbles from side to side'.

* **Old pot and pan** – *old man*. Used for a husband of long standing and suggestive of a certain domestication. An old couple will have mastered the art of how to *take and give*, which is to say *live* (and specifically live together). It is a neat play on the traditional response to the question often asked of long-married couples, 'What's the secret to staying together?': 'It's all about give and take. I give and (s)he takes.'

* **Pall Mall** – *gal*. Used in the context of a young man 'stepping out' with a gal. Pall Mall itself is one of the finest streets in London's St James's district and owes its name to a previous incarnation as a venue for matches of pall mall, a game not dissimilar to croquet.

* **Pride and joy** – *boy*. A rhyme echoing with parental delight in their progeny. Also used is *Rob Roy*, after Rob Roy MacGregor, the great flame-haired Scottish hero of the early part of the eighteenth century who played a pivotal role in the Jacobite uprising against William of Orange. While his story may have earned him little glory among the citizens of the English capital, his name is nonetheless synonymous with courage, heart and derring-do.

* **Ribbon and curl** – *girl*, particularly a young one of the sort likely to sport the hair styling described in the rhyme. In a variation on a theme, *twist and curl* might also be used. Another alternative is *ivory pearl*, suggesting someone of great beauty and highly valued.

* **Skin and blister** – *sister*. A distinctly unflattering description for one's nearest and dearest.

* **Soap and lather** – *father*. Perhaps stemming from the shaving ritual that most children witness their fathers engaging in at some point.

* **Soap and water** – *daughter*. A rhyme suggestive of the more fragrant nature (and fundamentally higher standards of hygiene) of the female sex.

SLANG IN ACTION

My old *soap* warned me about Kate. But I was young, and proud to call her my *jam tart*. On the day we got wed, I don't think there'd ever been such a sweet-looking *mother's pride*. And for a year we never had a cross word. But that all changed, soon as she found we were going to have a *basin*. As it turned out, it was twins. One *ribbon* and one *pride*. Two *jacks*, though. Since then, me and the *trouble* do nothing but fight.

Translation

My old *father* warned me about Kate. But I was young, and proud to call her my *sweetheart*. On the day we got wed, I don't think there'd ever been such a sweet-looking *bride*. And for a year we never had a cross word. But that all changed, soon as she found we were going to have a *baby*. As it turned out, it was twins. One *girl* and one *boy*. Two *brats*, though. Since then, me and the *wife* do nothing but fight.

—◊—

China plates – *Mates*. A classic of Cockney rhyming slang. 'You all right, me old china?' remains a question that can be regularly heard in the pubs of east London, having first been recorded on the city's building sites in the latter years of the Victorian era.

—⚏—

After his family, a proper London geezer will value nothing more highly than his *chinas*: here are some more phrases concerned with friendships, both their ups and downs.

* **Brussels sprout** – *Boy Scout*. The establishment of the Scouting movement in 1908 provided myriad new opportunities for socializing and building friendships.

* **Bubble Bath** – *laugh* (as in 'having a laugh'), requiring a pronunciation of 'barf'. An alternative is Steffi Graf, a nod to the former tennis champion from Germany. Alternatively, *cow and calf* or *bobble hat and scarf*.

Darby and Joan

Essentially, there's just no fun to be had *on your Darby and Joan* (that is to say, *on your own*). Darby and Joan are the epitome of companionship, an aged married couple who see out day after uneventful day together, so the rhyme is somewhat ironic. Whether Darby and Joan were real people is not known for sure, but they first appeared in fictional form in a poem by Henry Woodfall published in 1735 in the *Gentleman's Magazine*. It is said that Woodfall was employed at the time by a John Darby, who was married to a Joan. His poem, 'The Joys of Love', included the lines: 'Old Darby, with Joan by his side / You've often regarded with wonder. / He's dropsical, she is sore-eyed / Yet they're never happy asunder.'

* **Bushel of coke** – *bloke*. A bushel is a unit of dry volume equivalent to eight gallons. The phrase comes from the days when coke was understood as coal and not as a fizzy brown drink or a dangerous narcotic.

* **Bushey Park** – *lark*. Bushey Park is a well-to-do area in Hertfordshire, not far out of London.

* **Harbour light** – *right*. Used in the sense of 'all right'.

* **Lemon squeezer** – *geezer*.

* **Mile End** – *friend*. Mile End is an area of east London that was once home to the Queen's Hall, opened by Queen Victoria in 1887, to provide entertainment, leisure and

educational facilities to local residents. The neighbourhood was badly bombed in the Second World War, and was the site of the first V-1 attack.

* **On your Jack Jones** – *on your own*. A variation on the *Darby and Joan* phrase, and increasingly finding favour over it. There was probably no particular Jack Jones on whom the rhyme is based but one may now regularly hear heated arguments ending with one party going home to leave the other *on their jack*. Alternatively, some slang-speakers use *Tod Sloan* (leaving people *on their tod*). Sloan was a US jockey who had a short but illustrious career in horse racing on both sides of the Atlantic between the late 1880s and 1901, when he became caught up in an unfortunate betting scandal. It is a particularly appropriate choice, as there can be few more solitary places than the saddle of a horse.

* **Queens Park Ranger** – *stranger*. Queens Park Rangers (or the Hoops) are a west London football team who play at Loftus Road in Shepherd's Bush. Once friends, Cockneys should aim never to become Queens Parkers.

* **Saveloy** – *boy* (as in lad). An honourable mention for the saveloy, which continues to serve as the final instalment of many a boys' night out even in the face of competition from the kebab.

What is a Cockney?

A Cockney is a Londoner born within the sound of Bow Bells (see box on p. 151). Which areas are in earshot of the pealing bells is a fiercely contested question. It has been estimated that before the London skyline was cluttered with skyscrapers and the city lived under a permanent din of traffic, the noise could be heard six miles to the east, five to the north, four to the west and three to the south. On that basis, Cockneys could be born in as disparate locations as Hackney Marshes, Lambeth and Camden.

There are several theories about the origin of the term 'Cockney'. One theory says that when William the Conqueror and the Normans invaded in 1066 they nicknamed London the Land of Sugar Cake, or in their own language, Pais de Cocaigne. It was this word 'Cocaigne' that some have argued became 'Cockney' over the years. Others suggest different origins. In the fourteenth century Geoffrey Chaucer wrote in The Canterbury Tales of a 'cockenay' as a rather wimpish milksop-type figure and this became a popular term among the citizens of rural areas to describe namby-pamby city-dwellers. Londoners at some stage decided to embrace the word, after which it evolved into a term symbolizing urban, working-class pride.

In recent years we have witnessed the rise of the Mockney – a 'mock Cockney'. Usually hailing from the middle class and, at best, the outskirts of London, the Mockney seeks to give the impression of having Cockney roots, usually by adopting a dodgy accent and a smattering of slang. Early exponents, such as Blur's lead singer, Damon Albarn (admittedly born in Whitechapel but brought up in leafy Essex), realized the error of their ways and backtracked but others – notably Guy Ritchie (born in Hertfordshire the son of an advertising executive) – have made a long and prosperous career out of it.

Lyrics from a popular old song, 'I'm a Cockney Born in Bow' (author unknown)

Up the apples an' pears,
Through the Rory O'Moore,
Back to the dear old trouble an' strife
On the Cane an' Abel, I shall see
A pair o' Jack the Rippers an' a cup o' Rosie Lee

SLANG IN ACTION

It was my birthday and all I wanted was a cheeky half with my *chinas*. I was well up for a night down the Crown and Anchor. So I was heading home after work when Dave rang me and said he was going to have to work late. Next it was Pete who said he'd forgotten he had football training. Then Mike called to say he was doing a salsa class with the missus. 'You're having a *bubble*,' I said, all grumpy. 'I'm going to be on my *jack* on my birthday!' At that moment I opened the front door, and they all jumped out. 'Surprise!' they screamed. That's proper *miles* for you.

Translation

It was my birthday and all I wanted was a cheeky half with my *mates*. I was well up for a night down the Crown and Anchor. So I was heading home after work when Dave rang me and said he was going to have to work late. Next it was Pete who said he'd forgotten he had football training. Then Mike called to say he was doing a salsa class with the missus. 'You're having a *laugh*,' I said, all grumpy. 'I'm going to be on my *own* on my birthday!' At that moment I opened the front door, and they all jumped out. 'Surprise!' they screamed. That's proper *friends* for you.

GATES OF ROME: HOME

Gates of Rome – ***Home***. The giant gates (*porta*) built into the walls of ancient Rome would have beckoned in countless returning military heroes from far-off foreign lands.

Whether you're a centurion or a Cockney barrow boy, home is always where the heart is.

CAT AND MOUSE – **House**

A natural choice of rhyme given that the two creatures often do battle for the same domestic space.

Here is a selection of words on a domestic theme.

* **Apples and pears** – *stairs*. One of those slang expressions that the world and his wife knows.

* **Artful Dodger** – *lodger*. Referencing the streetwise child pickpocket (real name Jack Dawkins) in Charles Dickens's *Oliver Twist*. His own lodgings, shared with the criminal gang managed by Fagin, were far from exemplary. Alternatively, *Jolly Roger*, after the skull-and-crossbones flag flown by pirate ships, perhaps implying a certain distrust of the stranger living in your property. The rhyme also harks back to the figure of Roger the Lodger, a popular personification of sexual voraciousness ('roger' being slang for the sex act). Take, for instance, the following limerick: 'There was a young maid from Cape Cod / Who thought children came only from God. / 'Twas not the Almighty / Who pulled up her nightie, / 'Twas Roger the lodger, the sod.'

* **Aunt Maria** – *fire* (as in 'source of domestic warmth'). Sometimes replaced by *Ave Maria*.

* **Black Maria** – *fire* (in the sense of an uncontrolled blaze). Black Maria is the name given to a police vehicle used for transporting prisoners. There is, thus, the idea here of a destructive fire started deliberately.

* **Bob Hope** – *soap*. Bob Hope was a comedian, actor and performer and one of the twentieth century's biggest stars. He was born in Eltham, south London, moving to the USA only when he was four. Incidentally, his first show on American network radio was called the *Woodbury Soap Hour*.

25

* **Bride and groom** – *broom*. The rhyme may have taken some inspiration from the ritual traditional to several cultures of a bride and groom 'jumping the broom'.

* **Cain and Abel** – *table*. A mid-Victorian rhyme recalling the sons of Adam and Eve, whose relationship ended in murder.

* **Charley Mason** – *basin*. It is not certain that the rhyme is based on any specific individual, though there was a Charlie Mason who played for Wolverhampton Wanderers in the 1880s, including the 1889 FA Cup final, and appeared for England three times.

* **Dog and bone** – *telephone*. Another of the classics of the rhyming slang lexicon. In the days before the world mumbled through mobiles, phone receivers did bear a passing resemblance to a bone. An alternative rhyme is *trombone*, an instrument which (with a little squinting) can claim a certain similarity to old-style telephones and also brings to mind another slang expression for the phone, the *blower* (see Percy Thrower, p. 28).

* **Duke of Kent** – *rent*. After a man one might suspect does not have to overly worry about such matters. Alternatively, *Burton on Trent* after the town in Staffordshire with a long tradition of ale brewing. Here an association is thus forged between rent money and beer money.

* **Enoch Powell** – *towel*. Recalling the former Conservative MP whose name will forever be associated with the debate on immigration. In light of the provocative speech he made in 1968, perhaps he wanted his towel to mop up his predicted Rivers of Blood.

* **Funny feeling** – *ceiling*. Anyone who has ever laid on a bed a little the worse for wear and stared at the ceiling as the room spins around them will shudder at this rhyme.

* **Harry Randall** – *handle*. The same rhyme is used for a *candle* too. Randall, born in Holborn in 1857, was a music hall and pantomime star. His 1930 autobiography, *Old Time Comedian*, is considered one of the most enlightening insights into life on the vaudeville circuit ever written.

* **Hat and scarf** – *bath* (requiring the pronunciation 'barf'). Perhaps harking back to the days when a dip in a lukewarm tin bath was the best many could hope for.

* **Knobbly knee** – *key*. Knobbly knees became a minor working-class obsession for a while in the twentieth century as the focus of seaside holiday camp competitions. An understandable rhyme, given the uneven profile of a key.

* **Little brown jug** – *plug*. No doubt originating from the drinking song written by Joseph Winner in 1869 in celebration of spousal alcohol abuse. Its lyrics include: 'Me and my wife live all alone / In a little log hut we call our own; / She loves gin and I love rum, / And don't we have a lot of fun! / Ha, ha, ha, you and me, / Little brown jug, don't I love thee!'

27

* **Little Nell** – *bell*. Little Nell was Nell Trent, the tragic heroine of Charles Dickens's 1841 novel, *The Old Curiosity Shop*, who ultimately suffers a death guaranteed to strain the readers' tear ducts. The rhyme thus offers a pun on 'knell' and the solemn ringing of bells for a funeral.

* **London Bridge** – *fridge*. There can be no more London-y rhyme. Originally a wooden bridge was built by the Romans across the Thames around AD 50, it has been rebuilt and developed countless times since. The current incarnation was opened by Elizabeth II in 1972.

* **Merry old soul** – *coal*. A simple play on the nursey rhyme 'Old King Cole', with its lines: 'Old King Cole was a merry old soul, / And a merry old soul was he.'

* **Mona Lisa** – *freezer*. The most recognizable painting on the globe, produced by Leonardo da Vinci between 1503 and 1519. An alternative rhyme is an even cooler customer, *Julius Caesar*, the brilliant military leader who expanded the Roman Empire's dominance in Gaul and made the first incursions into Britain. He became a virtual dictator before his murder by political rivals on the Ides of March, 44 BC.

* **Percy Thrower** – *blower* (as in telephone). Thrower was a horticulturalist who gained wide exposure on various BBC shows, including *Gardeners' World* and as the architect of the Blue Peter garden.

* **Richard Burton** – *curtain*. A rhyme most likely referring to the Welsh-born twentieth-century actor rather than the nineteenth-century English explorer. Burton the actor was a hell-raiser touched with genius who was nominated seven times at the Oscars but never won. He was five times married (twice to Elizabeth Taylor).

* **Ronnie Biggs** – *digs* (as in accommodation). Biggs is the Lambeth-born criminal best known for his involvement in the 1963 Great Train Robbery, in which over £2 million was stolen and the engine driver, Jack Mills, beaten with an iron bar. Biggs spent many years holed up in Brazil before returning to serve a portion of his prison sentence in 2001.

* **Rory O'More** – *floor* (and also *door*). Colonel Rory O'More was one of the leaders of the Irish Rebellion in 1641 and gives his name to a bridge in Dublin. The same name was also used for the hero of a ballad (1826) and novel (1837) by the Irish writer Samuel Lover,

* **Semolina** – *cleaner*. Paying homage to the wallpaper paste-like pudding made from milk, sugar and grain that has haunted countless childhoods over many centuries.

* **Shovel and broom** – *room*. A 1920s successor to the rhyme *birch broom*, which in days of yore would have been used to keep a house clean.

* **Sir Walter Scott** – *pot*. An unlikely commemoration of the great man of Scottish letters, though he did spend his last years in debt, a condition summed up in the phrase 'without a pot to piss in'.

* **Tommy Trinder** – *window*. A rhyme demanding the
  Cockney pronunciation 'winder'. Born in Streatham,
  south London, Trinder was a great of British comedy, his
  popularity peaking between the 1930s and 1950s. Also
  used (especially for windows plural and again relying on
  an adapted pronunciation) is *Polly Flinders*, star of the
  nursery rhyme that runs: 'Little Polly Flinders / Sat
  among the cinders, / Warming her pretty little toes.' (*Polly
  Flinders* is sometimes used as a rhyme for *cinders* too.)

* **Trafalgar Square** – *chair*. Trafalgar Square is perhaps the
  most famous of all London squares and is home to
  Nelson's Column, a fitting monument to the great
  Admiral's victory against the Napoleonic forces at the
  Battle of Trafalgar in 1805. Having stood atop his column
  since 1843, Nelson might himself fancy a chair and a five-
  minute sit-down. An alternative rhyme is *Vanity Fair* after
  the 1848 novel by W. M. Thackeray.

* **Uncle Ned** – *bed*. A rhyme that also suggests the
  metaphorical description of sleep as 'the Land of Nod'.
  Cain fled to the original Land of Nod, according to the
  Book of Genesis, after killing Abel.

* **Vancouver** – *hoover* (as in the eponymic brand of vacuum
  cleaner). Vancouver is the largest city of the Canadian
  province of British Columbia.

* **Weeping willow** – *pillow*. One might easily imagine a quick
  forty winks beneath the pendulous branches of just such a
  tree on a river bank in summer time.

DOLLY VARDEN – **Garden**

Dolly is a character in Charles Dickens's 1841 novel *Barnaby Rudge* (set at the end of the eighteenth century), the beautiful daughter of Gabriel and Martha Varden. In the 1870s there was a fad for retro women's fashions during which time a certain sort of bustled, brightly coloured dress came to be known as a Dolly Varden. It inspired a song by Alfred Lee that contained the following lines: 'Have you seen my little girl? She doesn't wear a bonnet. / She's got a monstrous flip-flop hat with cherry ribbons on it. / She dresses in bed furniture just like a flower garden / A blowin' and a growin' and they call it Dolly Varden.' An alternative, and rather less interesting, rhyme is *beg your pardon*.

—⚬—

* **April showers** – *flowers*. Recalling the old maxim 'April showers bring May flowers.'

* **Baden-Powell** – *trowel*. Born in Paddington, London in 1857 Robert Baden-Powell was the British hero of Mafeking, the founder of the Cub Scout movement and a man who truly understood the joys of the great outdoors.

* **Lord Lovell** – *shovel*. The rhyme possibly refers to the ballad *Lord Lovel*, which first appeared in print around 1770. Alternatively, it might relate to the English aristocratic Lovell family. Francis, 1st Viscount Lovell was a noted ally of Richard the Third.

* **Old iron and brass** – *grass*. Recalling the memorable chant of the rag and bone man, preserved for ever in the music hall song 'Any Old Iron', written by Charlie Collins, E.A. Sheppard and Fred Terry.
* **Uncles and aunts** – *plants*.

SLANG IN ACTION

The mortgage was so much on our *cat* that we had to get an *artful*. A nice chap – always keeps his *shovel* neat. Only, one day he left the toaster on and it started a *black*. He was in the *hat* at the time, up the *apples*. The smoke was so bad he had to jump out of a *tommy*. He squashed all my *aprils* and *uncles* in the *dolly*. So we've put his *duke* up from next month.

Translation

The mortgage was so much on our *house* that we had to get a *lodger*. A nice chap – always keeps his *room* neat. Only, one day he left the toaster on and it started a *fire*. He was in the *bath* at the time, up the *stairs*. The smoke was so bad he had to jump out of a *window*. He squashed all my *flowers* and *plants* in the *garden*. So we've put his *rent* up from next month.

—◊◊—

TOOTING AND TIDDLYWINK: FOOD AND DRINK

Food and drink make up a rich part of our lives so it is unsurprising to find they are responsible for much colourful slang.

TOOTING – **Food**

Tooting is a contraction of Tooting Bec, an area of south London on the outer reaches of the Northern Line. The rhyme harks back to a word for food much in vogue among the thieving classes of the sixteenth century, *peck*.

—w—

We all need *Tooting* (or alternatively *in the mood*, or in *the nude* for the more daring), even if you're on a *Brixton riot* (*diet*). The question is, what to have? Here are a few ideas.

Lillian Gish – **Fish**

After the famed twentieth-century American star of stage, screen and television, whose career spanned seventy-five years.

* **Bessie Braddock** – *haddock*. A rhyme based on a post-war Labour MP for Liverpool whose waistline, some cruelly noted, suggested a penchant for a good fish supper.

* **Colonel Blimp** – *shrimp*. After the 1930s newspaper cartoon character created by David Low and the epitome of Little Englanders everywhere.

* **Frankie Vaughan** – *prawn*. After the much-loved Liverpool-born singer.

* **Grannies (Granny's wrinkles)** – *winkles*.

* **Jack the Ripper** – *kipper*. Recalling the unknown man responsible for at least five murders in the city's East End during the 1880s. Its usage brings to mind particularly grim images of filleting.

* **Jane Russells** – *mussels*. A tribute to the screen goddess that manages to link, admittedly a little tenuously, the image of seashells and bra cups, the latter of which she so famously and amply filled.

* **Richard Todd** – *cod*. After the British actor famed for movies including *The Dam Busters*.

* **Tommy Steeles** – *eels*. Those serpents of the River Thames so beloved of Londoners throughout the ages. Steele himself was one of the city's biggest stars, a Bermondsey boy who topped the hit parade in the 1950s with numbers like 'Singin' the Blues' to become the first great home-grown rock 'n' roller.

Hands and Feet – **Meat**

* **Bags of mystery** – *sausages*. One of the best examples of non-rhyming Cockney slang that, in one short phrase, leaves you to ponder just exactly what has been swept up off the abattoir floor and put into your good old-fashioned *banger* (or Bernhard Langer, as fans of Germany's greatest ever golfer have had it in recent years).

* **Billy Button** – *mutton*. Based on a fairly ancient nickname for an itinerant tailor.

* **Bubbly jock** – *turkey*. One for traditionalists, with the rhyme relating to *turkey jock*, an antiquated name for a male turkey.

* **Charlie Dicken** – *chicken*. An inelegant mangling of the name of Charles Dickens, maybe Britain's greatest novelist and certainly the finest chronicler of its capital city.

* **Dr Crippen** – *dripping*. A macabre allusion to the mild-mannered Hawley Harvey Crippen, the GP convicted of killing and chopping up his wife before burying her behind the walls of their Camden home in the early 1900s.

* **Duchess of York** – *pork*. A slightly unkind rhyme that has come to replace the older *knife and fork*.

* **Gillie Potters** – *pig's trotters*. Refers to a much-loved humorous BBC broadcaster of the 1930s, although the fading popularity of both him and the dish in question are likely to see this rhyme disappear altogether.

London Food

The classic Cockney dish is a bowl of jellied eels, though admittedly it is something of an acquired taste. It has helped keep Londoners fed since the eighteenth century, when eels were plentiful in the Thames and so cheap that even the poor could afford them if they could were not able to catch some themselves.

Preparation involves chopping the eels into chunks and then boiling them in a seasoned and slightly spicy stock. They are then allowed to cool, a process during which they jellify. They are sold in the city's pie and mash houses, of which there are still some eighty across the capital. The oldest establishment still going is Goddard's Pie Shop, which opened in 1890 and moved to its current site in Greenwich in 1952. While the shops still thrive, the eel has faired rather less well – just fifty were caught in the Thames in 2009.

* **Itchy teeth** – *beef*. Remember to say 'teeth' as 'teef', like a proper Cockney.

* **Joe Blake** – *steak*. Joe Blake seems to have been an imaginary figure created for the rhyme. Also acceptable is *Veronica Lake*, inspired by the Hollywood starlet of the 1940s. *Rikki Lake* might serve in the twenty-first century.

* **Kate and Sidney** – *steak and kidney*. A slightly imperfect but charming spoonerism.

* **Trolley and tram** – *ham*. Bringing to mind two popular means of darting around London in days gone by.

* **Uncle Sam** – *lamb*. A rhyme entirely unrelated to the personification of the American spirit.

Uncle Reg – **Veg**

* **Billy Cotton** – *rotten*. After the London-born band leader whose long career culminated in the Billy Cotton Band Show, which broadcast on BBC radio between 1949 and 1968.

* **Cockles and mussels** – *Brussels sprouts* (or simply *Brussels*). A rhyme seemingly designed to cause confusion.

* **Corns and bunions** – *onions*. Not one likely to increase your appetite for the veg in question.

* **Kings and queens** – *beans*.

* **Navigator** – *potato* (we're talking '*potaters*' in the East End). Refers to the 'navvies' who toiled on Britain's burgeoning rail and canal networks during the nineteenth century, with many of the labourers hailing from Ireland, a country particularly associated with the veg in question. You could also use *rosebud* (*spud*).

* **Polly Parrots** – *carrots*.

* **Woolwich and Greenwich** – *spinach*. Name-checking two famous areas of south London. The first syllable of Greenwich has to be pronounced 'Grin-', rather than the now commonly heard 'Gren-'.

* **Yous and Mes** – *peas*.

Other Useful Vocabulary

* **Apples and rice** – *nice*.

* **Army and Navy** – *gravy*.

* **Borrow and beg** – *egg*. Originally dreamt up in the Victorian era and given a new lease of life in the Second World War when shortages meant you would have to do just as the rhyme suggests to obtain any in significant numbers.

* **Bowl the Hoop** – *soup*. Harks back to the Victorian era when young scamps and urchins entertained themselves by wheeling a metal hoop along the roads.

* **Cough and splutter** – *butter*. Also *Calcutta*, after the former capital of the British Raj.

* **Drum and fife** – *knife*. The rhyme is usually contracted to *Drummond* and alludes to musical instruments commonly found in military bands. An alternative rhyme is *man and wife* (perhaps suggestive of a couple at daggers drawn . . .).

* **Duke of York** – *fork*. Duke of York is a title traditionally bestowed on the second son of the British monarch. An alternative rhyme is *roast pork*, a sumptuous delight to find upon your fork

* **Harry Tate** – *plate*. The music hall star of the rhyme is also used as slang for *late*.

* **High stepper** – *pepper*. Dating from the First World War. The term high-stepper – literally, a horse taught to walk with its hooves held high – was used colloquially for a fashionable person with a proud bearing.

* **Holy Ghost** – *toast*.

* **Lee Marvin** – *starving*. Not one of the most convincing rhymes, referencing the American actor who won an Oscar for *Cat Ballou* in 1965.

* **Lorna Doone** – *spoon*. After R.D. Blackmore's novel of 1869, *Lorna Doone: A Romance of Exmoor*.

* **Needle and thread** – *bread*.

* **Ruby Murray** – *curry*. After a beloved Irish singer whose heyday was in the 1950s with hits such as 'Softly, Softly', 'Heartbeat' and 'Evermore'. With curry being, apparently, the nation's favourite food, she is better remembered now as a slang term than as a recording artist.

* **Slap and tickle** – *pickle*. A rather frisky rhyme for a distinctly unsexy condiment.

* **Squad Halt** – *salt*. A verbal play on a military command.

* **Tommy Tupper** – *supper*. The rhyme is a slight mangling of Tommy Tucker, recalling the nursery rhyme which includes the lines: 'Little Tom Tucker / Sings for his supper. / What shall we give him? / White bread and butter.'

* **Waterloo (Battle of Waterloo)** – *stew*.

* **Yellow silk** – *milk*. A much more poetic rhyme than some.

Of course, in older, simpler days, you could string together any number of random slang phrases safe in the knowledge that no hot potato (*waiter* – remember, you'll need to pronounce the word as 'potater') would take you literally. In this age of Heston Blumenthal and his chums, you'll need to be a bit more wary . . . But if you mug up on all this, you should have no problems getting yourself a lovely, little *Lilley & Skinner* (the name of a famous bootmaker's shop opened in 1835 that was adopted as the slang for *dinner*)!

TIDDLYWINK – Drink

A creation of *Punch* magazine in the late nineteenth century, complete with a nod to the idea that certain drinks might leave the imbiber on the tiddly side of things. The word was originally used to mean a beer shop.

—✦—

These are all terms related to drinking of the non-alcoholic variety. Booze gets looked at in greater detail in the Rub-a-dub chapter, p. 55.

* **Dog and pup** – *cup*.

* **Everton toffee** – *coffee*. Everton toffee is a tooth-challenging sweet produced in the Everton district of Liverpool since the 1850s. Indeed, Everton Football Club boasts the nickname of the Toffees, with a Toffee Lady distributing sweets before every home game.

* **Fisherman's daughter** – *water*. A simple rhyme on an aquatic theme.

* **Geoffrey Chaucer** – *saucer*. Chaucer is one of the great names of English literature, who lived from *c.* 1343 to 1400 and whose great work was *The Canterbury Tales*. As the pilgrims told their stories at the inn, we may assume very few of them were supping their drinks from a cup and saucer.

* **Hansel and Gretel** – *kettle*. *Hansel and Gretel* is a German fairy tale most famously told by the Brothers Grimm, recounting the story of a brother and sister abandoned by their parents and kidnapped by a witch. They end up cooking her as they make their bid for freedom and might have made good use of a kettle in the preparation of an accompanying gravy.

* **Orinoko** – *cocoa*. Presumably a straightforward (if slightly corrupted) reference to the Orinoco River that flows for 1,300 miles through Colombia and Venezuela. Others, though, have suggested its roots are actually in a short novel called *Oronooko* written by Aphra Behn in 1668, one of the first novels in the English language.

* **Rosie Lee** – *tea*. It is often said that this rhyme pays homage to Rosie Lee Hovick, better known as Gypsy Rose Lee, a Washington-born burlesque dancer whose memoirs were made into the hit movie *Gypsy*. However, this bit of slang dates from the 1920s when Rose was but a small girl, so the connection is tenuous at best.

SLANG IN ACTION

We were *lee marvin* so we decided to get some *lillian* and chips. We ordered a *bessie*, two *richards* and half a roast *charlie*, three chips, two *slapped corns* and some mushy *yous*. I wanted a *slapped borrow* but it looked *billy* so I didn't. Uncle Jack doesn't have his own teeth so sucked the innards out of his *kate and sidney* pie, then slurped his *rosie* out of the *geoffrey*. Put me right off my *tommy*.

Translation

We were *starving* so we decided to get some *fish* and chips. We ordered a *haddock*, two *cods* and half a roast *chicken*, three chips, two *pickled onions* and some mushy *peas*. I wanted a *pickled egg* but it looked *rotten* so I didn't. Uncle Jack doesn't have his own teeth so sucked the innards out of his *steak and kidney* pie, then slurped his *tea* out of the *saucer*. Put me right off my *supper*.

LORD MAYORING: SWEARING, INSULTS AND BANTER

Lord Mayoring – Swearing. Something one might never expect to hear from the Lord Mayor of London, a post in existence since 1198 and most famously held by Dick Whittington four times between 1397 and 1419. (*Rip and tear* is an alternative rhyme for *swear*.)

—⚒—

Much of the language here is earthy, to say the least, and some of it grossly offensive. Several of the entries (in particular the homophobic slurs) are thankfully heard much less often today than in earlier decades.

* **Alphonse** – *ponce*. A phrase that became current in the 1950s to refer to a pimp. It has subsequently come to be used in reference to anyone who profits off the backs of others.

* **Barge and tug** – *mug* (as in a fool or a dupe). An alternative rhyme is *steam tug*, both phrases suggesting origination among London's dockers.

43

* **Berkeley Hunt (berk)** – *cunt*. 'Berk' has found its way into fairly common and polite(ish) usage, its colourful slang history unknown to most speakers. It is pronounced by slang-speakers to rhyme with 'work' but in 'Berkeley' it is pronounced to rhyme with 'lark'. The Berkeley Hunt, based in Gloucestershire, is among the oldest hunts in the world, dating back to the twelfth century. The Hunt's double life as slang for one of the harshest words in the English language may well owe something to age-old class resentments. An alternative rhyme is *James Blunt*, the name of one of the most successful recording artists of the twenty-first century, whose hit 'You're Beautiful' has been used as the first dance at countless weddings. Similarly, *Sir Anthony Blunt*, another well-known personality whose surname left him a sitting target for rhymers. Blunt was an art historian who became Surveyor of the King's Pictures before being unmasked as a Soviet spy (along with Philby, Burgess and Maclean), guaranteeing a level of exceptional unpopularity among the public.

* **Brandy butter** – *nutter*.

* **Cobblers' awls** – *balls* (as in *testicles*). A cobbler is a shoemaker and repairer, and an awl is a tool used for punching holes in leather or sewing heavy materials together. The phrase is usually shortened to just 'cobblers' and is most commonly used as an exclamation of disbelief ('What a load of cobblers!').

* **Crown and anchor** – *wanker*. A rhyme that uses a common pub name for its inspiration. Crown and anchor is also a dice game long popular in the British Navy and there may be an association between the act of shaking dice and the recognized 'wanker' hand gesture. Also *merchant banker*, reflecting a long-held distrust of all those who work in the banking world.

* **Doris Day** – *gay*. Day, born Doris Kappelhoff in 1922, found success in movies such as *Pillow Talk* and as a recording artist. Famous for her all-American wholesome image and perky attitude, she has long served as a gay icon. Also *C&A*, after the chain of clothing stores that were a feature on British high streets from the 1920s until 2001. Selling fashion at low prices, it had a reputation as cheap and cheerful.

* **Edna May** – *On your way!* Used to encourage the hasty departure of an unwanted presence. Edna May was a New York-born actress who wowed audiences in her native city and in London during the Edwardian era

* **Elephant and Castle** – *arsehole*. A slightly imperfect rhyme referencing an area in the London Borough of Southwark. Its unusual name derives from a coaching inn located in the vicinity from at least the mid-eighteenth century.

* **Ginger beer** – *queer* (a widely used synonym for a homosexual in days gone by). A rhyme that plays on the supposed effeminacy of the (non-alcoholic) drink in

45

question. Also used is *Brighton Pier*. Brighton, the much-loved seaside town on the Sussex coast and the home of the flamboyant Royal Pavilion built by George IV during his regency, has long been a thriving centre of British gay culture.

* **Haddock and cod** – *sod*.

* **Iron hoof** – *poof*. From an era when horses, and thus horseshoes, were a common sight in London.

* **Keith Moon** – *loon*. A well-chosen rhyme that pays tribute to the legendary drummer with *The Who* who had a reputation for outrageous alcohol- and drug-fuelled antics, including (supposedly) the driving of a Cadillac into a hotel swimming pool. He died in 1978 aged 32 after an overdose. Alternatively, *Man in the Moon*, a rhyme redolent of the 1960s when space travel was all the rage.

* **King Dick** – *thick*. Previously a rhyme for 'brick', so a natural progression in light of the phrase 'thick as a brick'.

* **Lump and bump** – *chump*. A mildly affectionate rhyme which suggests ungainly clumsiness and silliness.

* **Marbles and conkers** – *bonkers*. A fairly gentle term of abuse for someone considered to be a little mad. Marbles and conkers are both popular playground games (though conkers has increasingly fallen foul of health and safety regulations) and this slang is probably the root of the phrase 'to lose your marbles' (to go mad).

* **Miss Fitch** – *bitch*. Based on a non-specific Miss Fitch.

* **Pheasant plucker** – *fucker*. A cheeky spoonerism based on a tongue-twister with a refrain of: 'I'm not the pheasant plucker / I'm the pheasant plucker's son / And I'm only plucking pheasants / Till the pheasant pluckers come.'

* **Piccadilly** – *silly*. A reference to the London street that runs between Hyde Park Corner and Piccadilly Corner and home to some of the most expensive shops and hotels in the world, including the Ritz and Fortnum & Mason. The rhyme suggests a suspicion that extravagant displays of wealth reflect a lack of common sense, as in the old maxim 'A fool and his money are soon parted'.

* **Pony and trap** – *crap*, in the sense of something being of low quality ('That new song by James Blunt is pony'). An appropriate rhyme considering the detritus left on roads by the said animal pulling its vehicle.

* **Radio Rental** – *mental* (here generally understood as disconcertingly unstable). Radio Rentals was a once-familiar high street chain retailing audio-visual equipment but packed up business several years ago. The rhyme lives on.

* **Raleigh bike** – *dyke* (originally a derogatory term for a lesbian that has now, to some extent, been reclaimed by certain individuals of that sexuality). Raleigh is a long-established make of bicycle and the rhyme brings to mind the highly offensive use of 'bike' for a sexually promiscuous woman ('She's the village bike – all the boys have had a ride on her').

47

* **Ruck and row** – *cow*. A term of abuse directed exclusively at a woman that the speaker considers to be notably unpleasant. The slang rhyme alludes to the disputes likely to ensue between insulter and insultee.

* **Salvation Army** – *barmy*. The Salvation Army was established in 1865 by William Booth as the East London Christian Mission. Its quasi-military structure and its aims of doing charitable work while spreading the Christian gospel no doubt struck some observers as eccentric. Alternatively, *Dad's Army*, an affectionate nod to the Home Guard that worked so diligently during the Second World War, despite a reputation for haphazardness and eccentricity (a view cemented by the success of Jimmy Perry and David Croft's legendary sitcom *Dad's Army* that ran from the late 1960s until the mid-1970s).

* **Sharper's tool** – *fool*. A sharper was a confidence trickster and one of his primary tools would have been dice.

* **Tickle your fancy** – *nancy*. Yet another contribution to the canon of homophobia with a fairly weak hint of innuendo.

* **Top hat** – *pratt*. A piece of slang reflecting the working-class suspicion that the moneyed classes (that is to say, those who wore top hats) are prone to stupidity.

SLANG IN ACTION

I'm not really the sensitive sort but when some *piccadilly barge* started giving it the 'Big I am', it drove me *radio rental*. He was *king dick* and all. So I told him, 'You're talking *pony*, you *lump*.' 'It's you who's spouting *cobblers*,' he comes back at me. He had a look in his eye now, like he was a bit of a *brandy*. '*Marbles*,' I muttered under my breath. Then I gave him a shove and told him, '*Edna May*, you *top hat*!'

Translation

I'm not really the sensitive sort but when some *silly mug* started giving it the 'Big I am', it drove me *mental*. He was *thick* and all. So I told him, 'You're talking *crap*, you *chump*.' 'It's you who's spouting *balls*,' he comes back at me. He had a look in his eye now, like he was a bit of a *nutter*. '*Bonkers*,' I muttered under my breath. Then I gave him a shove and told him, '*Go away*, you *pratt*!'

—⚡—

NIGHT AND DAY:
PLAY AND LEISURE

Night and Day – *Play*. A mid-Victorian coinage that can be used in the sense of a dramatic production or to describe any activity designed for enjoyment and recreation. Perhaps the original rhymer had just returned from a particularly long production of *Hamlet* or something equally endurance-sapping.

—⚉—

Here is a selection of vocabulary related to leisure time and cultural pursuits: in terms of extent there is no comparison with the language devoted to going to the pub or playing sports!

* **Captain Morgan** – *organ* (as in musical instrument). Welsh-born Henry Morgan was a notorious pirate captain who operated in the Spanish Main. He lived out his final days as a wealthy man and something of a folk hero, dying in 1688. His name was used for a popular brand of rum in the 1940s.

* **Charlie Brown** – *clown*. The most likely origin is a popular song written by Jerry Lieber and Mike Stoller and

released by The Coasters in 1959. Entitled 'Charlie Brown', its lyrics run 'Charlie Brown, Charlie Brown / He's a clown, that Charlie Brown'.

* **Ding-dong** – *song*. Dating from the mid-nineteenth century, it is often used in the sense of a *sing-song* or group warble.

* **Fleas and itches** – *the pictures* (as in the cinema). The rhyme perhaps refers to the dangers of spending too much time in the cheap seats.

* **Hale and hearty** – *party*. A rhyme that engenders a sense of well-being and fine-fettle, just as a good party should.

* **Hey-diddle-diddle** – *fiddle* (as in violin). Relating to the nursery rhyme featuring the cat, the fiddle, and the eloping dish and spoon.

* **Hobson's Choice** – *voice*. The Hobson referred to is Thomas Hobson, a stable owner in the late sixteenth/early seventeenth centuries. He had well over forty horses but anyone wishing to hire a ride had to take the one in the nearest stall. Thus Hobson's choice is something appearing to be a free choice but where only one option is available.

* **Jacket and vest** – *West*. If a proper Cockney wants a good night out he might decide to 'go up West', which is to say he'll make the short trip into the West End. On such a trip he is likely to dress up in his best bib and tucker, which might help to explain this particular rhyme.

* **Joanna** – *piano* (requiring the pronunciation 'pianah'). A rhyme, dating from the 1840s, that recalls the days when every decent boozer had a *Joanna* in the corner, and a crowd relishing a good knees-up.

* **Kick and prance** – *dance*. Revealing an unsophisticated but not uncommon attitude to the art form. An alternative is *south of France*, a nineteenth-century rhyme rich in promise of the exotic and sophisticated.

* **Mangle and wring** – *sing*. In the days before automatic washing machines, wet clothing was passed through a mangle and wrung out. Here there is a definite sense of someone 'mangling' a song.

* **Roger Mellie** – *telly* (as in television). A comic creation from the team behind *Viz* magazine, a publication which revels in its rudeness. Roger's catchphrase is a succinct 'Bollocks!' An alternative rhyme is *Mother Kelly*, on whose doorstep Nellie and Joe sat in George A. Steven's 1925 song, 'On Mother Kelly's Doorstep'.

* **Stewed prune** – *tune*. A Victorian effort, the rhyme redolent with joylessness.

Music Hall

As you will have noticed, an extraordinary number of rhyming slang phrases have their origins in the names of popular music hall performers.

Music hall as an art form is all but dead now but between *c.* 1850 and *c.* 1950 it was among the most popular forms of entertainment in the country, bridging the gap between the saloon bar entertainments introduced in certain pubs from the 1820s and the shows that were offered by the expensive (and distinctly classist) established theatres. One of the great centres of saloon bar entertainment was the Eagle pub, which lay just off the City Road in north London and which crops up in a nursery rhyme 'Up and down the City Road / In and out The Eagle / That's the way the money goes / Pop goes the weasel.'
The first music hall is generally considered to be the Canterbury, which opened in 1852 on Westminster Bridge Road in Lambeth and offered a similar bill of fare to such pubs – usually a mixture of comic and sentimental songs, comic skits and novelty acts (incorporating everything from acrobats, magicians and mesmerists to strongmen, jugglers and ventriloquists). In music halls, rather than facing the stage in theatre-type stalls, audiences were often seated in a cabaret style and could drink and smoke in an informal atmosphere (so much so that some became legendary for their rowdiness, capable of bringing down all but the toughest of performers).

SLANG IN ACTION

We love a good knees-up down at the social. Friday night it's a proper old *hale*. Frank sits down at the *joanna*, knocking out the *ding-dongs* while Beryl *mangles* along. She's got a great *hobson's*, even though she's no spring chicken. Some weeks Alf joins in on the *hey-diddle-diddle* and that's lovely but if Bert says he wants to have a go on his *captain morgan*, we have to say no. He's a bit *mutton*, you see, and it ruins it.

Translation

We love a good knees-up down at the social. Friday night it's a proper old *party*. Frank sits down at the *piano*, knocking out the *songs* while Beryl *sings* along. She's got a great *voice*, even though she's no spring chicken. Some weeks Alf joins in on the *fiddle* and that's lovely but if Bert says he wants to have a go on his *organ*, we have to say no. He's a bit *deaf*, you see, and it ruins it.

—⁓—

RUB-A-DUB: THE PUB

Rub-a-dub – *The Pub*. A rhyme dating from the last decade of the nineteenth century, inspired by an old nursery rhyme: 'Rub a dub dub / Three men in a tub / And who do you think they be? / The butcher, the baker, / The candlestick-maker / Turn 'em out, knaves all three!'

—◊—

The *Jack tar (bar)* is today as much a focal point of social life as it ever was (Jack tar was a common nickname for a seaman, since sailors used tar to weatherproof their clothes and strengthen rigging; the rhyme also acknowledges the seagoing man's reputation for drinking).

PICK AND CHOOSE – Booze

The rhyme suggests the myriad types of alcohol available. An alternative is *River Ouse*. There are two rivers with that name in England, one in Sussex (in which the author Virginia Woolf drowned herself) and the other in the north-east. Some rhymers opt instead for *mud and ooze*.

* **Amos and Andy** – *brandy*. *Amos 'n' Andy* was a situation comedy (the lead characters performed by Charles Correll and Freeman Gosden) that proved hugely successful on US radio from the 1920s until the 1950s. The alternative is *fine and dandy*, the feeling the drinker hopes to experience.

* **Andy Pandy** – *shandy*. Andy Pandy was the marionette star of *Watch with Mother* in the 1950s. Dressed in a blue-and-white-striped all-in-one number, the character was rather emasculated. Shandy has a similar reputation among the boozers of London.

* **Brahms and Lizst** – *pissed*. A somewhat cultured rhyme for a notably uncultured state. Johannes Brahms, the German Romantic composer, met Franz Liszt, his Hungarian counterpart, in Weimar, Germany, in 1853.

* **Bright and frisky** – *whisky*. A classic 'cause and effect' rhyme (at least for the first tot or two).

* **Britney Spears** – *beers*. A rhyme of recent vintage, celebrating the troubled American pop star. Meanwhile *Christmas cheer* is sometimes used for a singular *beer*, suggestive of high spirits and goodwill.

* **Currant cakes** – *the shakes*. A rather too cute rhyme for the unpleasant condition of delirium tremens.

* **Didn't ought** – *port*. A gentle play on the unconvincing protestations of the 'reluctant' tippler.

* **Eighteen carat** – *claret* (blood). The rhyme is a classification of high-quality gold.

* **Elephant's trunk** – *drunk*. A mid-Victorian rhyme on several levels; not only is the elephant able to take on vast volumes of liquid in its trunk but the 'pink elephant' is the archetypal image of a drunken hallucination.

* **Finger and thumb** – *rum*. The rhyme suggests the depth of a good shot.

* **Giggle and titter** – *bitter*. An allusion to some of the potential effects the drink might have on the drinker.

* **Mother's ruin** – *gin*. A very old rhyme, recalling gin's 'golden age' in the eighteenth century when there were over 7,000 gin joints in the capital, selling the spirit so cheaply that it became the drink of choice for the working classes. The rhyme points to the social damage caused. An alternative rhyme is *Vera Lynn*.

* **Philharmonic** – *tonic*. Possibly because the mixer helps bring out the finer notes in a spirit.

* **Plinkety plonk** – *wine*. A slightly obscure rhyme, taking the French *vin blanc* (white wine) as its subject. Almost always contracted to *plonk*, it is understood to refer to wines of all type.

* **Quentin Tarantino** – *vino* (as in wine). Tarantino is the director of such landmark movies as *Reservoir Dogs* and *Pulp Fiction*, films awash with blood (or, as you might say in slang, *claret*).

* **Runner and rider** – *cider*. A rhyme from the turf, the term denoting a horse and jockey entered into a race.

57

* **Sugar and spice** – *ice*. A tasty rhyme for a subject utterly lacking in taste.

* **Woolwich Ferry** – *sherry*. The Woolwich Ferry has been transporting passengers (some 2.5 million per year these days) between the north and south banks of the River Thames since 1889.

SMOKING

* **Blind man's buff** – *snuff*. Perhaps reflecting the effect that a pinch of strong snuff can temporarily have on the taker's eyesight as their eyes water.

* **Cherry ripe** – *pipe*. Recalling a poem by Robert Herrick from 1648. Cherry wood was also a material favoured by the manufacturers of pipes.

* **Colney Hatch** – *match*. An area in the London Borough of Barnet that became notorious for its lunatic asylum built in the mid-nineteenth century.

* **Cough and drag** – *fag* (as in cigarette). A pretty accurate depiction of the act of smoking.

* **Cuts and scratches** – *matches*. A rhyme dating from the Victorian era.

* **La-di-dah** – *cigar*. Perhaps suggesting that cigars are the preserve of the upper classes.

* **Laugh and joke** – *smoke*. Echoes the case often argued by smokers that smoking is a sociable activity.

* **Vera Lynn** – *skin* (as in cigarette paper). Resulting in the unlikely sight of countless stoners wandering around to ask all and sundry if they've 'got any veras'. After Vera Lynn, the lady who sang 'White Cliffs of Dover' and was the nation's sweetheart during the Second World War.

ILLEGAL SUBSTANCES

* **Boutros Boutros-Ghali** – *charlie* (as in cocaine). A rhyme from the 1990s when Boutros-Ghali became director general of the UN.

* **Jack and Jills** – *pills*. A fairly cynical hijacking of the children's nursery rhyme characters. That the original Jack and Jill spent time going up and down hills ties in with the idea of 'uppers' and 'downers' (that is to say, mood-affecting drugs).

* **Lou Reed** – *speed* (as in amphetamine). Lou Reed was the lead singer of The Velvet Underground, one of the great New York bands of the 1960s and 1970s. He went on to have a successful solo career and had a reputation for extravagant narcotic abuse.

* **Ollie Reed** – *weed*. Reed was an actor well known as a bon viveur and *enfant terrible*, though his name is more associated with alcohol than any mind-altering drug.

* **Uncle Mac** – *smack* (as in heroin). Another hijacking of a figure from childhood innocence. Uncle Mac was Derek McCulloch, a BBC broadcaster who made programmes

for youngsters from the 1930s to the 1960s. He was also the voice of Larry the Lamb.

DYNAMITE – **Fight**

A rhyme redolent with a sense of power and destructiveness.

However good-naturedly a night out might begin, too much booze can see it descend into trouble; rhyming slang has more than its fair share of words related to fighting, tension and conflict.

* **Aristotle** – *bottle*. As discussed elsewhere, Aristotle is the root of the slang *arris* (for *arse*) but in this context is the rhyme for *bottle* in the sense of *courage*.

* **Barney Rubble** – *trouble*. Barney is the neighbour and best friend of Fred in the long-running Stone Age cartoon *The Flintstones*. The two often found themselves in scrapes. The rhyme works particularly well as 'barney' has been used to mean a row or fight since the nineteenth century.

* **Bull and cow** – *row*. While the cow might by and large be docile, the bull is the embodiment of aggression.

* **Frankie Howerd** – *coward*. What you don't want your friends to be if you find yourself in a corner. While no aspersions should be cast on Mr Howerd's personal courage (although he was a notable victim of stage fright), his act was filled with nervous stuttering and exclamations of 'Oooh, no, missus'.

* **Half-ouncer** – *bouncer*. An ironic rhyme considering most bouncers offer rather more of a challenge to the scales.

* **Mr Hyde** – *snide*. A remarkably fitting literary allusion, recalling Edward Hyde, the pernicious alter ego of Dr Henry Jekyll in Robert Louis Stevenson's haunting novella of 1886.

* **Newington Butts** – *guts* (as in courage). Newington Butts is an area in the London Borough of Southwark now most associated with a stretch of the A3 near Elephant and Castle. The 'Butts' part of the name may hark back to an earlier time when the area served as an archery butts (or practice field).

* **Ocean liner** – *shiner* (as in black eye). Also used is *Morris Minor*, the much-loved and affordable car that remained in production from 1948 until 1971.

* **Oliver Twist** – *fist*. Recalling Charles Dickens's creation who, though small in stature, had the heart of a fighter.

* **Pat and Micked** – *licked* (as in beaten in a fight). Here Pat and Mick are generic Irish navvies who doubtless know how to handle themselves in a fight.

* **Read and write** – *fight*. A rhyme using cerebral activities to denote something far more corporeal.

* **Rotten Row** – *a blow* (as one might receive in a fight). Rotten Row is the name of the track that runs along the southern reaches of London's Hyde Park. Laid out by William III in the seventeenth century it was never rotten

but was rather a hangout where the rich and influential could take the air together.

* **Scapa Flow** – *go* (as in flee). A body of water near the Orkneys in Scotland and Britain's chief naval base during the First and Second World Wars. Also a pun on *scarper* (to depart in haste) from the Italian *scappare* (to escape).

* **Two and eight** – *state* (as in heightened emotional condition). A situation more likely to arise after having had a skinful.

* **Uncle Bertie** – *shirty* (as in angry and ill-tempered). It is etymologically unclear why Bertie is so narked.

WEST HAM

Founded in 1895 as Thames Ironworks, West Ham (otherwise known as the Hammers or, by real supporters, the Irons) play at the Boleyn Ground in Upton Park. Decked out in distinctive claret and blue, the club has put its fans through the wringer over the years. There have been glory days, notably three FA Cups and in 1965 a European Cup Winner's Cup. Many great players have appeared for them, including folk heroes such as Billy Bonds, Trevor Brooking and Paolo di Canio. It was also the team of Bobby Moore, Martin Peters and Geoff Hurst, three pivotal figures in England's World Cup win of 1966, leading Irons fanatics to claim that it was actually West Ham that won the trophy.

---

* **West Ham Reserves** – *nerves*. West Ham is *the* club of the East End (see box opposite) and was bound to find a place in the local lingo. The club's performances being somewhat up and down, no doubt the Reserves have tried the nerves of many a fan.

SLANG IN ACTION

So there I was standing at the *jack*, just about to order. *Britneys* for me and Dave, an *andy* for Trevor and a *vera and philharmonic* for his bird. Anyway, up comes this geezer, completely *brahms* on *runner*. He asks me for a *cough* so I tell him, sorry I don't *laugh* no more. That's when he got all *uncle bertie*. Luckily some *half-ouncer* waded in before there was a real *barney*. Wish I'd given the geezer an *ocean*, though.

Translation

So there I was standing at the *bar*, just about to order. *Beers* for me and Dave, a *shandy* for Trevor and a *gin and tonic* for his bird. Anyway, up comes this geezer, completely *pissed* on *cider*. He asks me for a *fag* so I tell him, sorry I don't *smoke* no more. That's when he got all *shirty*. Luckily some *bouncer* waded in before there was real *trouble*. Wish I'd given the geezer a *shiner*, though.

—⁓—

A DAY AT THE BELT
AND BRACES:
SPORT AND GAMBLING

The belt and braces – **_The races_**. British racecourses have long been places to see and be seen, with strict dress codes adhered to. This rhyme gives a nod to such sartorial matters.

As can be seen from the vocabulary below, a large proportion of the slang connected with sports and games is rather more concerned with gambling than active participation.

* **April Fools** – *football pools*. In an age before the National Lottery, most get-rich-quick schemes involved staring at the previous week's football results in the hope of being able to predict score draws in the following weeks matches. Filling in the coupon for the Aprils was a weekly ritual in many households and, in general, never came to anything.

* **Billy Bunter** – *punter*. After the rotund and myopic anti-hero of Frank Richard's *Greyfriars* novels. It suggests a highly ambiguous attitude towards gamblers.

* **Charles Dance** – *chance*. After the highly respected English actor and director.

* **Charlie Drake** – *break* (as in a 'scoring visit to the snooker table'). After the pocket-sized English comedian (1925–2004) born in Elephant and Castle.

* **Cream cookie** – *bookie* (as in 'bookmaker').

* **George and Ringo** – *bingo*. George Harrison and Ringo Starr might have considered their lucky numbers had come up when they hit the big time with the Beatles.

* **Grumble and mutter** – *flutter* (as in a 'bet'). A rhyme picking up on the sounds emitted by a disgruntled punter after his hot tip has limped in last.

* **Holy Ghost** – *starting/winning post*. A long-standing symbol of blind faith for gamblers.

* **Horses and carts** – *darts*. Dating from the early part of the twentieth century.

* **Hot dinner** – *winner*. The rhyme suggests what one might be able to afford after a successful visit to the bookies.

* **Iron horse** – *racecourse*. The rhyme recalls a phrase used to describe early traction engines at a time when they were yet to displace horse-drawn vehicles in moving people and cargoes around the country. The slang is also used for dog tracks.

* **Lambeth Walk** – *chalk* (as used in snooker, pool and billiards). Referring to a hit from the 1937 musical *Me and*

My Girl, written by L. Arthur Rose and Douglas Furber, with music by Noel Gay. Performed by Lupino Lane, the song-and-dance routine became a sensation.

* **Nanny Goat** – *the Tote*. The Tote (short for the Horserace Totalizator Board) was established by the British government in 1928 to regulate horse race gambling, much of which had been operating outside the law.

* **National debt** – *bet*. A wry acknowledgement of how gambling can seriously harm your bank balance.

* **Nose and chin** – *win*. A horse race might well be decided by a distance as short as a nose and a bet placed 'on the nose' is for an outright win.

* **Rasher and bubble** – *a double* (as scored in darts). The rhyme refers to the breakfast favourites of a rasher of bacon and bubble-and-squeak (fried potatoes and leftover greens) – a diet that few sports other than darts will happily support. The importance of the double in darts is captured in the words of one of its east London-born legends, Bobby George: 'Trebles for show and doubles for dough.'

* **Rats and mice** – *dice*.

* **Smoked haddock** – *paddock*.

* **Struggle-and-strainers** – *trainers*. Amusing recognition of the plight of the rookie keep-fitter. An alternative is *Claire Rayners*, in honour of the late nurse, writer and broadcaster, better known for her kindly advice as an agony aunt than for her sporting prowess.

This Sporting Life

The sporting community has provided us with much specialized language and slang. For the average Cockney, sport is likely to play a significant part in life. A few sports have become especially associated with Cockney London, football, inevitably, commanding the greatest attention, with West Ham the definitive team of the East End.

Over the years boxing has also become intrinsically linked with the Cockney, partly down to the presence in Bethnal Green of York Hall, one of the country's premier boxing venues. Many great champions have been born within the sound of Bow Bells, and the Kray twins both had brief professional careers before turning to other 'business'. Among their first commercial interests was a snooker club, again in Bethnal Green. Often played in dark, smoke-filled and airless rooms, London's snooker halls have borne witness to many a dubious deal and unpleasant altercation.

Those with a penchant for gambling were able to go to the dogs (sometimes metaphorically as well as literally), with Walthamstow Stadium for a long while one of London's most popular venues and immortalized on the cover of the 1994 album *Parklife* by Blur, who were famous Mockneys (see pp. 21–22). The stadium hosted its last race in 2008.

Darts has also produced a few slang phrases and for a while in the 1980s the sport's greatest player was indisputably the Hackney-born Eric Bristow, who proudly bore the nickname of the Crafty Cockney.

* **Tommy Dodds** – *odds*. A rhyme with a complex history rooted in a coin-tossing game of the nineteenth century, which in turn spawned a music hall song with the lines: 'Heads or tails are sure to win / Tommy Dodd, Tommy Dodd.' From these origins, it took a small leap of imagination to come to this slang rhyme.

* **Typewriter** – *fighter* (as in boxer). An odd choice of rhyme, considering that most boxers tend to do their talking with their fists.

COLDSTREAM GUARDS – Cards

(As in playing cards.) The Coldstream Guards are a regiment of the British Army, founded by General George Monck in 1650. No doubt many a soldier has passed the time with a hand or two of cards.

—◊—

* **Baked Bean** – *queen*. And a somewhat less fitting rhyme for his wife. Also used is *Mary Green*, not based on any known person but possibly coined while Queen Mary was consort of George V (r.1910–36).

* **Cats face** – *ace*. Aces usually being strong cards to hold, the cat's face is presumably a grinning one in the manner of the Cheshire Cat featured in *Alice's Adventures in Wonderland*.

* **Gold ring** – *king*. A suitably regal rhyme.

* **Jam tarts** – *hearts*. A rhyme bringing to mind Lewis Carroll's *Alice in Wonderland*, featuring the Queen of Hearts who made some tarts and the knave who stole them.

* **Lemonades** – *spades*. Those desirous of a drink providing more energy have added the alternative rhyme of *Lucozades*.

* **Rub-a-dub-dub** – *clubs*. Referencing the popular nursery rhyme with the three men in a tub.

* **Simple Simons** – *diamonds*. One of the less convincing rhymes, referencing the nursery rhyme in which Simon doesn't even have a penny for a pie so is unlikely to be able to afford a sparkler.

SNOOKER

There are established rhymes for all the colours in snooker except, strangely, the white and the green. A challenge, perhaps, for the modern rhymers out there.

* **Bald head** – *red* (the ball worth one point). Suggestive of a pate that has spent rather too long in the sun.

* **Cinderella** – *yellow* (requiring a pronunciation of 'yellah'; the ball worth two). Referencing the folk tale told in many cultures throughout time of a put-upon young lady who comes through to marry her handsome prince. It is hard to imagine she spent much time in a snooker hall herself.

* **Half-a-crown** – *brown* (the ball worth four). After a pre-decimalization coin equivalent to 2/- 6d.

* **Danny la Rue** – *blue* (the ball worth five), after the famous drag artist. Born as Daniel Carroll in Cork in 1927, he was one of the biggest draws on the London cabaret scene by the 1960s and went on to find a bigger audience through regular television appearances. He died in 2009.

* **Rinky dink** – *pink* (the ball worth six). Rinky dink started as American slang for something cheap and insignificant, so a slightly odd choice for one of the high-value balls in snooker.

* **Jumping jack** – *black* (the ball worth seven). A jumping jack is a child's toy, a figure usually made from wood with limbs that move energetically at the tug of a string. An alternative rhyme is *coalman's sack*, an item itself usually black with coal dust.

SLANG IN ACTION

Joe was always down at the *cream cookie's*. The sort of *billy* that they love – quick to have a *grumble* but never able to spot a *hot dinner*. Until one day he was at the *belt* and got friendly with a couple of *struggles*. They gave him a tip so he put a *national debt* on this nag to *nose*. *Tommys* of 250 to one. It romped home. Now he owns his own horse, which he named *Charles Dance*.

Translation

Joe was always down at the *bookies*. The sort of *punter* that they love – quick to have a *flutter* but never able to spot a *winner*. Until one day he was at the *races* and got friendly with a couple of *trainers*. They gave him a tip so he put a *bet* on this nag to *win*. *Odds* of 250 to one. It romped home. Now he owns his own horse, which he named *Chance*.

—◊◊◊—

HAROLD MACMILLANS:
A LIFE OF CRIME

Harold Macmillans – *Villains*. Macmillan was Conservative prime minister from 1957 until 1963 and famously announced that the British people had 'never had it so good'. While Macmillan retired from politics with few blemishes on his character, he had to deal with one or two rogues in his cabinet, not the least of whom was John Profumo. Macmillan's wife also had an affair with Lord Boothby, who would become a friend of the Krays in later years.

—⁂—

London has always had a reputation as a centre of crime, perhaps inevitably given the vast numbers of people who have fitted into such a confined geographical area. Where there is crime, there is secrecy, hence the need for secret languages, and the criminal underworld has proved one of the most fruitful birthing grounds for slang.

* **Babbling brook** – *crook*. An unlikely association forged between a calming pastoral image and a perpetrator of dodgy dealings.

* **Bottle of scent** – *bent* (as in corrupt). Perfume 'off the back of a lorry' is historically one of the staples of dodgy market traders.

The London Underworld

No part of London has had quite such a reputation for nefarious activities as the East End. In the period 1888–91 Whitechapel became the scene of between five and eleven brutal slayings at the hands of Jack the Ripper, whose identity remains a mystery to this day. Contemporaneously, Arthur Conan Doyle was capturing the imaginations of millions by sending his detective, Sherlock Holmes, deep into London's underworld, often in dark corners of the East End such as Limehouse (which had a reputation for opium dens).

More recently, the rise of the Kray twins, Ronnie and Reggie, and their gang (including their older brother Charlie) in the 1950s ensured that the East End would be forever associated with gangland crime. They dominated London's organized crime throughout the 1960s but after an investigation headed by the Met's Detective Superintendent Leonard 'Nipper' Read they were convicted of the brutal murders of two associates (George Cornell and Jack 'the Hat' McVitie) and given long sentences. Both were to die in prison. Reg Kray even published a *Book of Slang* in 1989, which he hoped would furnish the most accurate dictionary of criminal slang compiled up to that point.

* **Cornflake** – *fake*. Alternatively, *Sexton Blake* is used, after the fictional detective who first appeared in 1893 and cropped up in books and comics, and on radio and television until the latter part of the twentieth century. A sometime resident of Baker Street, at one stage a public poll suggested he was more famous than his spiritual forefather, Sherlock Holmes.

* **Daisy beat** – *cheat*. A rhyme of Victorian heritage, though its exact origins are somewhat unclear.

* **Eighteen pence** – *fence* (as in a 'dealer in stolen goods').

* **Half-inch** – *pinch* (as in 'to steal'). One of those rhymes that has moved across into the vocabulary of the population at large.

* **Hey-diddle-diddle** – *fiddle*. A straightforward reference to the nursery rhyme with the lyrics 'Hey diddle diddle, / The cat and the fiddle'.

* **Holy friar** – *liar*. Suggesting that perhaps even the words of the godly should not always be taken at face value. An alternative is *Dunlop tyre*, after the famous motoring name.

* **Joe Rourke** – *fork* (as in pickpocket). The term 'fork' was used to refer to pickpockets from as early as the eighteenth century. *Joe Rourke* is not believed to be modelled on a real person.

* **Johnnie Walker** – *talker* (in the sense of a grass). The rhyme references a popular brand of Scoth whisky, perhaps playing on the idea of demon drink loosening the tongue.

* **Pete Tong** – *wrong*. A rhyme from the 1990s when Pete Tong, a Radio 1 DJ and icon of the club scene, was at the peak of his popularity.

* **Pork pie** – *lie*. Though only firmly established in the lexicon in relatively recent decades, the concept of 'telling porkies' has captured the public imagination.

* **Punch and Judy** – *moody* (as in stolen goods). Punch and Judy are the puppet figures who can trace their histories back to the Italian *commedia dell'arte* and were re-envisaged in Britain as an end-of-pier entertainment. The anarchic activities of Punch make him something of a lawless figure.

* **Robin Hood** – *good*. Recalling one of the great folk heroes of English culture. He is evident in folkloric sources from the thirteenth century onwards and tales of his antics as he led his band of merry men in thieving from the rich to give to the poor continue to thrill to this day. His appearance in rhyming slang perhaps reflects the sometimes ambiguous relationship Londoners have had with certain criminals over the years.

* **Sorry and sad** – *bad*. A suitably sorrowful nineteenth-century effort. Alternatively, *Jack the Lad*, the personification of masculine swagger who first appeared in a song of 1840 that included the lines: 'If ever fellow took delight in swigging, gigging, kissing, drinking, fighting, / Damme, I'll be bold to say that Jack's the lad.'

* **Tea leaf** – *thief*. One of the most enduring of all Cockney rhyming slang phrases.

* **Whistle and toot** – *loot*.

THE JUSTICE SYSTEM

* **Barnaby Rudge** – *judge*. Rudge was the eponymous hero of a Charles Dickens novel of 1841, set during the Gordon riots of 1780. Rudge himself was something of a simpleton, which might be an accurate reflection of certain slang-speakers' attitudes towards judges.

* **Beecham's pill** – *Old Bill*. Beecham's Pills were a laxative first sold in the 1840s by Thomas Beecham, containing a mixture of soap, aloe and ginger. They remained in production until as recently as 1998. The origin of the name Old Bill for the police is disputed but may be related to the habit of seventeenth-century 'constables of the watch' (precursors to the modern Police Force) of carrying billhooks to use as weapons.

* **Birdlime** – *time* (as in a 'prison sentence'). Birdlime is a glue-like substance coated on to branches in order to capture certain species of feathered friend. Rhymers clearly appreciated this notion of capture and the phrase 'doing bird' is widely understood to mean serving a prison term.

* **Bladder of lard** – *Scotland Yard*. Lard is rendered animal fat and in days of old was stored in pig's bladders, hence this phrase of unusual grimness.

Porridge

Porridge was a sitcom by Dick Clement and Ian La Frenais that originally ran on the BBC from 1974 until 1977. It starred Ronnie Barker as Norman Stanley Fletcher, Richard Beckinsale as his cellmate Lennie Godber and Fulton Mackay as prison guard Mr Mackay. Fletcher was a London-born career criminal constantly at war with 'the system' but ultimately good-hearted. The title of the show is a reference to the non-rhyming slang 'doing porridge', a euphemism for being in prison (porridge long being the standard breakfast served up to inmates). Fletcher and his cohorts regularly sprinkled their conversation with slang of rhyming and non-rhyming types. In one scene Fletcher is playing Monopoly when he lands on a particular square and memorably exclaims, 'Would you Adam and Eve it? Go to jail!'

* **Bottle and stopper** – *copper* (itself long-established slang for a 'policeman'). Plays on the idea of 'stopper' as a person or thing that acts to prevent.

* **Bottle of wine** – *a fine*. Perhaps suggestive of a celebration when a custodial sentence was avoided.

* **Brass tacks** – *facts*. An imperfect but effective rhyme.

* **Brighton Rock** – *dock* (as in 'the defendant's enclosure in a courtroom'). Refers to the 1938 book by Graham Greene that used the criminal underbelly of the titular south coast town for its backdrop.

* **Bucket and pail** – *jail*. An appropriate rhyme considering the significance of the bucket in the prison ritual of slopping out.

* **Daily Mail** – *tale*. Suggesting a certain level of distrust in the national newspaper's journalistic integrity.

* **Dog's tooth** – *truth*. Possibly a pun on 'God's truth'. Dogs are also a symbol of faithfulness.

* **Flowery dell** – *cell*. A romantic and poetic imagining of an inmate's living quarters.

* **Garden gate** – *magistrate*. Some slang-speakers prefer to work with the informal word for a magistrate, 'beak'. This allows for the rhyme *bubble and squeak*, a dish off the menu in most prisons.

* **Harry Lauder** – *warder*. Harry Lauder was born in Edinburgh in 1870 and became one of the most popular figures of the music hall age, performing in full Scottish regalia.

* **Jackanory** – *story* (here understood as a 'tall tale' of the type sometimes heard in the dock). *Jackanory* is a BBC series that has run since 1965, in which guest readers narrate popular and classic children's stories. The title comes from a nursery rhyme of 1760: 'I'll tell you a story / About Jack a Nory. / And now my story's begun, / I'll tell you another / Of Jack and his brother. / And now my story is done.'

* **Jam roll** – *parole*. The convicts' hoped-for first meal on the outside?

* **Little Boy Blue** – *screw* (as in 'prison warder'). Another nursery rhyme reference, in which the boy in question 'looks after the sheep' while the inmates doubtless wish he was, metaphorically speaking, 'under the haystack, fast asleep'.

* **Newgate Gaol** – *tale* (of the type that might be heard from an old lag). This particular prison was in use from the twelfth century until 1902 and its location is now the site of the Old Bailey (the Central Criminal Court). Many convicts went straight from the jail to meet their ends on the scaffold. Also used is *weep and wail*, particularly in the sense of a story told to engender sympathy.

* **Noah's Ark** – *nark* (as in 'informer'). Dating from the end of the nineteenth century. Sometimes reworked as '*oah's nark*' ('*whore's nark*'), which gives an indication of the low esteem in which such a character is held by the criminal fraternity. A rather more common alternative name for an informer is *grass*, which has its roots in rhyming slang as well. It is a shortened form of *grasshopper*, which may have served as a rhyme for either *copper* or *shopper* in this context.

* **Royal Mail** – *bail*. A reference to the postal service that perhaps plays on the idea of bail being 'posted'.

* **Scooby Doo** – *clue*. After the canine star of the long-running Hanna-Barbera cartoon series. Scooby and his investigating chums have made a career out of not picking up on clues.

* **Shovel and pick** – *nick* (as in prison). The rhyme lists a couple of the tools that could be useful in a prison break.

* **Sweeney Todd** – *Flying Squad* (a branch of the London Metropolitan Police charged with investigating armed crime). Sweeney Todd is a fictional bogeyman who first appeared in the mid-Victorian era in a penny dreadful entitled *The String of Pearls*. The 'Demon Barber of Fleet Street' was in the habit of dispatching victims in his barber's chair before chopping them up to provide the fillings of the pies of his companion, Mrs Lovett.

TOOLS OF THE TRADE

* **April Fools** – *tools*. This was a term popular among nineteenth-century ne'er-do-wells to describe tools used in housebreaking. The rhyme may have been inspired by the idea of 'getting one over' on somebody else.

* **Fire alarms** – *firearms*. A rhyme that creates a suitable sense of danger and panic.

* **First aid** – *blade*. One of those knowing bits of slang in which the utilization of the rhyme object results in the need for the subject word. An alternative is *shovel and spade*, with its grim connotations of grave diggers.

* **Hot cross bun** – *gun*. A phrase that hardly captures the threat posed by its subject.

* **House of Fraser** – *razor* (particularly a cut-throat version).

Often contracted to *howser*. House of Fraser is the famous department store chain with its origins in Glasgow in the mid-nineteenth century.

* **Lady from Bristol** – *pistol*. A rhyme of uncertain pedigree.

* **Phil the Fluter** – *shooter* (as in a gun). Recalling a song by Percy French, in which Phil from Ballymuck hosts a joyous ball and entertains all with hs musical prowess. There is one mildly threatening line that asserts: 'Ye've got to pay the piper when he toothers on the flute.'

SLANG IN ACTION

Fred was always a bit of a *babbling, half-inching* anything that took his fancy. And most of what came out of his mouth was *porkies*. But I couldn't *adam and eve* it when some *bottle* picked him up with a *hot cross bun*. Before his feet could touch the ground Fred was in the *brighton* in front of a *barnaby*. He gave Fred a year but Fred says that's all right 'cos he likes it in his old *flowery* anyway.

Translation

Fred was always a bit of a *crook*, *pinching* anything that took his fancy. And most of what came out of his mouth was *lies*. But I couldn't *believe* it when some *copper* picked him up with a *gun*. Before his feet could touch the ground Fred was in the *dock* in front of a *judge*. He gave Fred a year but Fred says that's all right 'cos he likes it in his old *cell* anyway.

SMILE AND SMIRK: THE WORLD OF WORK

Smile and Smirk – Work. A rhyme that might imply work is a source of happiness or alternatively, under a different reading, that it is worthy of scorn.

—◊◊—

While there are a fair few expressions dealing with work, business and commerce, it is interesting to note that there are also several dealing with the absence of work, a problem that has often beset London's working classes.

* **Backseat driver** – *skiver*. Developing the idea of an annoying presence who won't themselves take on the job in hand.

* **Beeswax** – *tax*. There is a modern idiom 'Mind your own beeswax' (to mean 'Mind your own business'), giving this rhyme added resonance since few people are keen to have their tax affairs raked over. Meanwhile, *bees and honey* is slang for *money*.

* **Beggar-my-neighbour** – *labour exchange*. The labour exchange was the precursor to the modern job centre. Beggar-my-neighbour is a card game originating in the mid-nineteenth century and here evokes a sense of poverty and of going cap in hand amongst one's community.

* **Bright and breezy** – *easy*. The rhyme is almost the perfect description of the Cockney of popular lore, as in the lyrics of 'The Lambeth Walk': 'Everything's bright and breezy, / Do as you damn well pleasy.'

* **Couple of bob** – *job*. A couple of bob was the equivalent of two shillings in old money, thus bringing together the notions of labour and payment.

* **Daft and barmy** – *army*. A wry comment on attitudes towards the armed forces.

* **Dead loss** – *boss*. Slang offering a classic insight into labour relations.

* **Duck and dive** – *skive* (as in 'to shirk work'). The rhyme means to use one's ingenuity to avoid trouble – which in this context would seem to be a hard day's graft.

* **Gert and Daisy** – *lazy*. Gert and Daisy were a couple of BBC comedy Cockney char ladies from the 1930s to the 1960s played by real-life sisters Elsie and Doris Waters (their brother used the stage name Jack Warner and became hugely famous as Dixon of Dock Green).

* **Hedge and ditch** – *market pitch*. A rhyme from the late Victorian era popular among costermongers and bookies.

* **Joe O'Gorman** – *foreman*. There was, the evidence suggests, no specific Joe O'Gorman who inspired this bit of slang. However, London's building projects have long relied on imported labour from Ireland and so the name is perhaps representative of an archetype.

* **Last card of the pack** – *the sack* (as in redundancy). A rhyme suggestive of the game being up. Also plays on the tradition that you're 'given your cards' when sacked.

* **Mrs Mopp** – *shop*. Mrs Mopp was the office char lady character in the BBC radio show *It's That Man Again*, which starred Tommy Handley and ran from 1939 to 1949. Her catchphrase was, 'Can I do you now, sir?'

* **Office worker** – *shirker*. Another piece of social comment, rhyming slang traditionally being a language of dockers, manual workers and market traders.

* **Tea and toast** – *post*. Bringing together two classic features of the average weekday morning.

CROWN JEWELS – Tools

The rhyme elegantly suggests the great value of tools to the workman.

* **Benny Hill** – *drill*. Hill was a comedian and actor most famous for his cheeky-chappy character. He seemed to spend much of his career chasing or being chased by scantily clad young lovelies to the tune of 'Yakety Sax'.

* **Cock sparrow** – *barrow*. Cock sparrow also doubles as a Cockney term for a mate or chum (as in 'You OK, me old cock sparrow' or alternatively, 'me old cocker').

* **Elsie Tanner** – *spanner*. Elsie Tanner was a much-loved character from *Coronation Street*, played by Pat Phoenix from 1960 until 1984.

* **Leaky bladder** – *ladder*. Possibly referring to the effects that a particularly high climb can have on the uninitiated.

Costermongers

A costermonger is a name for a street seller of fruit, vegetables and assorted other produce. During their heyday in the mid-nineteenth century, there were crowds of costermongers throughout the capital, especially around the great markets like Covent Garden, Billingsgate, Spitalfields and Smithfield.

Relations between costermongers and the police were notoriously bad. The costermongers liked to regulate themselves and imposed their own forms of street justice when one of their number stepped out of line. They were less interested in involving the authorities and created their own languages in the interests of retaining confidentiality.

In his 1859 *Dictionary of Modern Slang, Cant and Vulgar Words*, John Camden Hotten wrote of the costermongers in hardly glowing terms, outlining their 'low habits, general improvidence, love of gambling, total want of education, disregard for lawful marriage ceremonies, and their use of a peculiar slang language'.

* **Monkey's tail** – *nail*.

* **Mother-in-law** – *saw*. Perhaps suggestive of things around which you should be wary.

* **Mrs Duckett** – *bucket*. Seemingly not related to a real person called Mrs Duckett.

* **Stutter and stammer** – *hammer*. An essential bit of slang for any West Ham fans.

BREAD AND HONEY – Money

While honey provides the rhyme, bread has a long association with money (for instance, in the terms 'dough' and 'earning a crust'). Also evokes the eighteenth-century nursery rhyme 'Sing a Song of Sixpence', with its lines 'The king was in his counting house, / Counting out his money; / The queen was in the parlour, / Eating bread and honey.'

—∿∿—

* **Boracic lint** – *skint*. Normally contracted to boracic (or, now disassociated from the original rhyme, represented sometimes as brassic). Lint soaked in boracic acid was a commonly used antiseptic dressing.

* **Bread and butter** – *gutter*. Where one finds oneself when out of money. A cruel twist on the *bread and honey* rhyme.

* **Goose's neck** – *cheque*.

* **Greengages** – *wages*. Green has long had an association with money. In Britain the old pound note was referred to as a green because of the colour of the paper on which it was printed, while in the USA, the dollar bill continues to be known as a greenback.

* **Halfpenny stamp** – *tramp*. Suggestive of stretched funds.

* **Iron tank** – *bank*. Evoking strength and impenetrability. Good for keeping money in, bad for getting money out.

* **Nelson Eddies** – *readies* (as in 'cash'). Nelson Eddy (1901–67) was a popular American singer with an exceptional baritone voice.

* **On the floor** – *poor*. Poetically evoking a sense of being down on one's luck and at a low ebb.

* **Peg-legger** – *beggar*. Conjuring up a Dickensian image of a one-legged old soldier leaning upon a crutch and appealing to passers-by for a penny or two.

* **Rhubarb pill** – *bill*. Rhubarb pills were a popular cure for constipation at the time this rhyme was coined in the late nineteenth century. Some bills, if large enough, presumably have a similar effect.

* **Rupert Bears** – *shares*. Rupert is the cartoon bear created by Mary Tourtel, becoming a household name in a regular *Daily Express* cartoon strip before branching out into books and television. His life seems joyfully unencumbered by financial concerns, though he is of course known for wearing checks.

* **Sausage roll** – *the dole* (that is to say, unemployment benefit). The sausage roll is historically a hearty dish affordable to almost all.

* **Sherbert dip** – *tip*. Recalling a favourite childhood sweet.

* **Stand to attention** – *pension*. As the rhyme suggests, this is slang that originated in the Army and referred explicitly to a serviceman's pension, though it has come to cover pensions in general.

* **Tomorrow** – *borrow*. A knowing rhyme suggestive of when a loan is always to be paid.

BANGERS AND MASH – Cash

Perhaps suggesting that sausage and mash represents the good life.

* **Abergavenny** – *penny*. After the market town situated in Monmouthshire in Wales.

* **Ayrton Senna** – *tenner*. After the Brazilian three-times Formula One World Champion who lost his life in a crash at the 1994 San Marino Grand Prix.

* **Bag of sand** – *grand* (as in a thousand pounds).

* **Charlie Clore** – *score* (as in twenty pounds). Sir Charles Clores was a noted British financier in the twentieth century who owned, among other interests, Selfridges.

He bequeathed a magnificent collection of painters by J.M.W. Turner to Tate Britain on London's Millbank.

* **Coal and coke** – *broke*. Implying poverty such that one cannot even afford to keep themselves warm.

* **Lady Godiva** – *fiver* (as in five pounds). Referencing the Anglo-Saxon heroine of Norman England who, according to legend, rode naked through Coventry to protest against unfair taxes.

* **Lost and found** – *pound*. A rhyme that suggests the 'easy come, easy go' nature of money.

* **Macaroni** – *pony* (as in twenty-five pounds). Pony has been slang for this sum since the eighteenth century though the origins of the term are oblique.

* **Nifty** – *fifty* (as in fifty pounds), the rhyme itself slang for smart and stylish.

SLANG IN ACTION

I've always *smiled*. Had loads of *couples*, not all of them *bright*. Never been a *backseat driver*. Paid my *beeswax*. Never had the *last cards*. Never had a boss who's thought I was *gert*. These days I work in a *mrs mopp*. Hardware. I specialize in *elsies*. Anything for a *greengage*. No better feeling than knowing you've always got a *lady* in your back pocket.

Translation

I've always *worked*. Had loads of *jobs*, not all of them *easy*. Never been a *skiver*. Paid my *tax*. Never had the *sack*. Never had a boss who's thought I was *lazy*. These days I work in a *shop*. Hardware. I specialize in *spanners*. Anything for a *wage*. No better feeling than knowing you've always got a *fiver* in your back pocket.

—⁓—

TATE AND LYLE: STYLE AND APPAREL

Tate and Lyle – *Style*. Refers back to the sugar-refining company formed in 1921 by the merger of the businesses of Henry Tate and Abram Lyle, who both entered the market in the mid-part of Queen Victoria's reign.

—w—

While money may not always have been in plentiful supply among London's working classes, pride in appearance has always been a core value.

* **Alan Whickers – *knickers*.** A tribute to the debonair broadcasting legend particularly famed for his reports from disparate corners of the globe. Benny Hill once ran a series of parodic sketches called 'Knicker's World'. Also *Brenda Frickers*, after the Dublin-born actress who won an Oscar in 1990 for the film *My Left Foot*.

* **Almond rocks – *socks*.** Almond rocks was a popular treat in the Victorian era, a sweet bisuit made with flaked almonds and candied peel.

* **Baked beans** – *jeans*. Levi 501s or Heinz 57s.

* **Canoes** – *shoes*. Drawing on the physical similarities between the two objects. For the generation brought up on the antics of the *Sex and the City* girls, there is an almost too convenient alternative in *Jimmy Choos*. Choo is perhaps the most famous living shoe-designer, alongside Manolo Blahnik, and operates out of London, having fostered a long association with Hackney. His products were objects of almost lustful desire for the character Carrie Bradshaw, played by Sarah Jessica Parker.

* **Charlie Prescot** – *waistcoat*. A rhyme relying on the antiquated pronunciation of waistcoat as 'westcot'. Modern users might prefer an updated *John Prescott*, after the former Labour deputy prime minister and a man built to model just such an item of clothing.

* **Daisy roots** – *boots*. Establishes the image of something planted firmly in the ground. Lonnie Donegan incorporated it into his song 'My Old Man's a Dustman': 'He looks a proper narner / In his great big hob nailed boots / He's got such a job to pull 'em up / That he calls them daisy roots.'

* **Dicky dirt** – *shirt*. A 'dickie' was the name for a detachable shirt front from the earliest days of the nineteenth century (perhaps linked to the coinage of 'dicky bow' for a bow tie). The addition of 'dirt' to make the rhyme work is suggestive of the dangers to a crisp white shirt in the grimy city.

* **Eddie Grundies** – *undies* (as in 'underwear'). Eddie Grundy is a character in BBC Radio 4's *The Archers*, the world's longest-running soap opera. Played by Trevor Harrison, Eddie is always working on some get-rich-quick scheme or other.

* **Epsom races** – *braces*. The most famous of all the races at Epsom Downs is the Derby, which has been run since 1780. Epsom is in Surrey, a short trip out of London, and the arrival of the railways allowed Londoners of all classes to dress up and make a day of it, a tradition that lives on.

* **Fag packet** – *jacket*. A jacket pocket is a natural home for a packet of ciggies.

* **Fleas and ants** – *pants*. Recalling the phrase 'ants in your pants'.

* **Fly-by-nights** – *tights*. While a fly-by-night is generally someone considered unreliable or of dubious trustworthiness in business, here there is also the sense of moonlit flits and of hosiery whipped off after dark.

* **Half and half** – *scarf*. The alternative, *tin bath*, relies on the pronunciation of 'bath' as 'barf'.

* **House of Lords** – *cords* (as in corduroy trousers). A fashion item rarely seen in the hallowed corridors of Parliament's Upper House.

* **Leg of mutton** – *button*. An alternative among scholars of cricket is *Len Hutton*, who played for Yorkshire, captained

England to Ashes victory and was among the most prolific batsmen of all time, scoring 364 in an innings against Australia in 1938.

* **Lionel Blairs** – *flairs*. Blair is a mildly camp actor, choreographer and dancer, perhaps best known for his many years as a team captain on the charades-based TV show *Give Us a Clue*. His eternal fame was secured by his being the subject of outrageous innuendo by Humphrey Lyttelton on *I'm Sorry I Haven't a Clue*.

* **Lucy Locket** – *pocket*. Referencing a nursery rhyme probably dating from the eighteenth century. Lucy was, it is believed, a real person – a barmaid at Fleet Street's Cock public house. The verse runs: 'Lucy Locket lost her pocket, / Kitty Fisher found it. / Not a penny was there in it, / Only ribbon round it.'

* **More or less** – *dress*. A cheeky nod, perhaps, to what might be on show depending on the particular cut and style of the dress.

* **Ooh-la-la** – *bra*. In which the corrupted French rhyme adds a quaint layer of sexual suggestiveness.

* **Pair of kippers** – *slippers*. Implicit is the notion of wafting foot odour. An alternative is *Yankee clipper*, a clipper being a speedy sailing ship popular with merchants in the nineteenth century (of which *Cutty Sark* docked at Greenwich is one of the finest examples). This latter rhyme continues the association between footwear and boats established above.

* **Peckham Rye** – *tie*. Peckham Rye is a neighbourhood of Southwark immortalized by Muriel Spark in her novel *The Ballad of Peckham Rye*. William Blake also claimed to have visions there.

* **Pound note** – *coat*. Perhaps pointing up that the more money you have to spend, the better the coat. An alternative is *Quaker oat*, a tribute to the popular breakfast cereal. As the wise know, on a cold day a good breakfast is what you need to set you up.

* **Reelings and rockings** – *stockings*. A frisky little rhyme born from Chuck Berry's rock 'n' roll classic 'Reeling and Rocking', with its suggestive boasts of 'reelin' and a-rockin' and rollin' till the break of dawn'.

* **Roman candles** – *sandals*. A type of traditional firework that also conjures up images of ancient Rome and its distinctive footwear.

* **Round the houses** – *trousers* (usually contracted to *round the's* or sometimes *round de's*). In a variation of Harris Weston and Bert Lee's classic 1938 song, 'Knees Up, Mother Brown', Fat Old Uncle Henry is depicted dancing while the buttons on his trousers come off one by one. It finishes with the lines: 'Another one went "pop", / He said I'm gonna keep on 'till me round the houses drop.'

* **Swallow and sigh** – *collar and tie*. Suggestive of a certain discomfort in dressing formally.

* **Tit-for-tat** – *hat*. Almost exclusively contracted to *titfer*.

* **Tomfoolery** – *jewellery*. Usually shortened to *tom* by nefarious sorts planning a spot of robbing.

* **Turtle doves** – *gloves*. Hailing from the 1850s, when the birds were considerably more common in Britain than they are now. Of course, my true love sent me a pair of them on the Second Day of Christmas. These days, a pair of gloves is a far more likely gift.

* **Weasel and stoat** – *coat*. A rhyme where the creatures in question on occasion find themselves recycled as the item of clothing they describe.

* **Whistle and flute** – *suit*. One of the most widely used of all slang phrases.

* **Widow Twankey** – *hanky* (as in 'handkerchief'). Widow Twankey is the traditional pantomime dame who has been appearing in the Aladdin story since 1861. Always played by a man, she is the mother of Aladdin and Wishy Washy and is normally the proprietor of a Chinese laundry, where she no doubt launders many a hanky.

Pearly Kings and Queens

To many, the Pearly Kings and Queens of London are symbols of 'Cockney London', famous for their distinctive outfits covered in pearl buttons and for mastery of rhyming slang. They serve as the heads of a charitable organization rooted in the traditions of the London working class. Today there is a king and queen for each London borough as well as for the City of London and the City of Westminster.

The organization traces its origins back to 1875 and an orphan, Henry Croft, who earned his living by sweeping the city's market streets. He was drawn to the coster-monger lifestyle, with its smart talk, distinctive fashions (pearl buttons were commonly sewn on to seams, pockets and hats) and sense of social responsibility (at least to each other). Having found gainful employment, Henry decided he wanted to do something to help the children in his old orphanage, so started to collect money for them as he worked. He kept an eye out as he swept for any buttons that had fallen off people's clothes and then sewed them on to his own clothes until his suit and hat were entirely covered. Even now, it is the Kings who are responsible for designing and making their outfits. Henry's great-granddaughter is the Pearly Queen of Somers Town to this day.

SLANG IN ACTION

Everyone knows Geoff. A big fellah, nice enough until someone upsets him. He always wears the same thing – great big *daisies* on his feet, a pair of classic *baked beans*, a white *dicky* and a smart black *weasel*. Always has a *titfer* on his bonce too. What people don't know is that underneath it all he's wearing *alans* and an *ohh-la-la* that belong to his wife. That's what I call *tate*.

Translation

Everyone knows Geoff. A big fellah, nice enough until someone upsets him. He always wears the same thing – great big *boots* on his feet, a pair of classic *jeans*, a white *shirt* and a smart black *coat*. Always has a *hat* on his bonce too. What people don't know is that underneath it all he's wearing *knickers* and a *bra* that belong to his wife. That's what I call *style*.

BIG EARS AND NODDY: BODY

Big Ears and Noddy – **Body**. Should a lady be passing through the East End, she may hear a cheeky chappy nudge his mate and comment, 'Have you seen the big ears on that?' This is not an observation on her *Toby jugs* (that's *lugs*, as in ears) but a compliment of sorts. Whether she is *needle and pin (thin)* or a bit *porky pig (big)*, chances are her form will catch the eye of someone or other.

—∞—

The human body has inspired a wealth of rhyming slang, from the cute to the utterly obscene, travelling south from the *loaf of bread (head)* all the way down to the *plates of meat (feet)*.

LOAF OF BREAD – Head

* **Apple pips** – *lips*. Sometimes *battleships* is used, particularly where the said lips are a medium for harsh words.

* **Barnet Fair** – *hair*. Barnet Fair, which continues to be held annually in a corner of north London, started during the

reign of Elizabeth I as a livestock fair. An alternative is *Alf Garnett*, a bigoted, West Ham-supporting east Londoner who appeared in the landmark sitcoms *In Sickness and in Health* and *Till Death Us do Part*. Played by Warren Mitchell, he was distinctly lacking in the hair department.

* **Boat Race** – *face*. The Boat Race has been contested annually by the rowing crews of the Universities of Oxford and Cambridge along the River Thames since 1856 (with the exception of the world wars). An alternative rhyme is *Chevy Chase*, recallling *The Ballad of Chevy Chase*, written no later than 1540, which tells the story of an unauthorized hunt led by the Earl of Northumberland that leads to a bloody skirmish between the English and the Scots. Other options include *glass case*, drawing a link between the human face and that of a watch or clock protected by a glass case. *Jem Mace* is an older variant, paying homage to a bareknuckle boxing champion of the nineteenth century whose nickname was 'Gypsy'. His own face presumably suffered considerable punishment over the course of his career.

* **Bottle of beers** – *ears*. A curiously ungrammatical little rhyme.

* **Crocodile** – *smile*. Bringing a mind a particularly toothy grin.

* **Cyril Lord** – *bald*. A rhyme that relies on the Cockney pronunciation of 'Lord' as 'Lawd' and 'bald' as 'bawld'.

Lord, having grown up among the textile mills of Lancashire, was in the middle decades of the twentieth century a famed owner of a carpet company (a 'rug' is often used as a slang term for a 'wig').

* **General Booth** – *tooth*. A reference to William Booth, the Methodist preacher who founded the Salvation Army and served as its general from 1878 until his death in 1912.

* **Gunga Din** – *chin*. Gunga Din was the eponymous heroic water-carrier in Rudyard Kipling's 1892 poem. With its famous last line (' Tho' I've belted you and flayed you, / By the livin' Gawd that made you, / You're a better man than I am, Gunga Din!'), there may be some connotation of the phrase 'Keeping your chin up'.

* **Hampstead Heath** – *teeth*. The Heath is one of the best-loved green areas in London, situated in the north of the city and providing some of its finest vantage points.

* **Jackdaw** – *jaw*. A rhyme dating to the mid-nineteenth century.

* **Just as I feared** – *beard*. A literary allusion to Edward Lear's poem, 'There was an Old Man with a Beard'. It features the stanza: 'There was an Old Man with a beard, / Who said, 'It is just as I feared! / Two Owls and a Hen, / Four Larks and a Wren, / Have all built their nests in my beard!' The slang is usually contracted to *just as*.

* **Mince pies** – *eyes*. First in circulation in the 1850s and one of the most enduring of all slang phrases.

* **Nanny goat** – *throat*.

* **North and South** – *mouth*.

* **Ocean wave** – *shave*. An alternative is *Chas and Dave*, a slightly ironic rhyme as neither Chas nor Dave ever sported much of a clean-shaven look.

* **Peashooter** – *hooter* (as in 'nose'). Conjuring up images of small boys propelling items from their nostrils.

Chas and Dave

Chas and Dave have been purveying their unique brand of Music Hall-tinged boogie woogie since 1975, creating a whole new genre of their own known as 'rockney'. Because of these Cockney associations and their liberal use of slang, they are often described as East Londoners, but in fact, Chas Hodges and Dave Victor were both born in North London.

One of their greatest hits was 'Gertcha', an older slang expression of uncertain meaning which serves as an exclamation of shock and surprise, along the lines of 'Get away!'. Chas and Dave spend the song discussing its deeper nuances: 'Well there's a word that I don't understand. / I hear it everyday from my old man. / It may be Cockney rhyming slang, / It ain't in no school book/ He says it every time that he gets mad, / A regular caution is my old dad.'

Some websites also claim that the band recorded a song called, suitably enough, *The Cockney Rhyming Slang Song*, although this author was sadly unable to trace a copy of it.

* **Ruby rose** – *nose*. Particularly suited for those in possession of a nose showing signs of a cold or, perhaps, of an over-fondness for the demon drink.

* **Salmon and trout** – *pout*. A rhyme of rare appropriateness, especially given the growing popularity of the phrase 'trout pout' to describe a certain look achieved by non-invasive plastic surgery.

* **Syrup of figs** – *wig*. An imperfect rhyme based on a substance commonly employed as a cure for constipation.

* **Toby jug** – *lug* (as in *ear*). Toby jugs were born out of the potteries of Staffordshire in the mid-eighteenth century, depicting seated figures with caricatured features.

* **Watch and chain** – *brain*. Creating a connection between the whirring cogs of a watch and the metaphorical cogs of the mind.

* **Whip and lash** – *moustache*.

BIG EARS AND NODDY – Body

* **Bow and quiver** – *liver*.

* **Bristol Cities** – *titties*. The classic slang for the female bosom, usually contracted to *Bristols*. It refers to one of the two football teams based in Bristol (Rovers being the other), thus linking two great traditional male loves – breasts and soccer. Quite why Bristol City, rather than say

the more famous Manchester City, should have become the established rhyme is unclear.

* **Cabman's rests** – *breasts*. Cabmen's rests were specially constructed shelters for slumbering cab operatives in the days of horse-drawn carriages open to the elements. Here there is perhaps a connection between the idea of rest and the image of the female bosom as a pillow.

* **Chalk Farm** – *arm*. Referring to a lively London district just north of Camden.

* **Darby Kelly** – *belly*. Often abbreviated to *Darby Kel*. What or who Darby was is not clear.

* **East and West** – *chest*. A non-gender-specific term for this area of the body. Indeed, the sense of broadness inherent in 'East and West' suggests the male physique. *Mae West* is a rhyme suited exclusively to the female physique, recalling one of Hollywood's earliest and greatest sex symbols. Her name pluralized predictably doubles for *breasts* and is also shorthand for a life-saving inflatable jacket.

* **German Band** – *hand*. German bands were groups of itinerant musicians who entertained the locals in London and many other British cities during the nineteenth century and into the early years of the twentieth. As an alternative, use *Margate Sands*, an imperfect rhyme recalling one of the favourite coastal retreats for Londoners during the heyday of the English seaside.

* **Haystack** – *back*. Used both for a human's back and for the back of anything in general. Also used is *Penny black*, introduced in 1840 as the world's first prepaid postage stamp, championed by Sir Rowland Hill who oversaw a comprehensive overhaul of the postage system.

* **Jamaica rum** – *thumb*. The drink was a staple for those whose livelihoods took them away to sea for long periods of time, whether with the Navy or on the commercial vessels seen in the London docks.

* **Limehouse Cut** – *gut*. The Limehouse Cut is a stretch of canal in east London, built in the seventeenth century and thus the oldest canal in the city.

* **Long and linger** – *finger*. The rhyme conjures up images of a lover's touch or perhaps even the delicate hand of a pickpocket lifting a wallet.

* **Raspberry ripples** – *nipples*. An equally juvenile rhyme.

* **Rock and boulder** – *shoulder*. Creating an image of strength and solidity.

* **Strawberry tart** – *heart*. A rhyme in which the chosen fruit prompts obvious comparisons in colour and shape with the internal organ.

* **Thrupenny bits** – *tits*. A thrupenny bit was a coin worth three pennies in pre-decimal Britain. Its use here might involve a juvenile comparison between the coins and nipples. As an alternative, there is *Brad Pitts*. A

straightforward rhyme utilizing one of the leading Hollywood stars of his generation, and a man long associated with beautiful women.

* **Worms and snails** – *fingernails*. A rhyme sure to put you off biting yours.

BIG BASS DRUM – Bum

A rhyme that serves as a joyful celebration of the callipygian figure.

The following vocabulary refers to the 'south of the waistband' regions and is not for the faint-hearted.

* **Birds and bees** – *knees*. *Biscuits and cheese* is also widely used.

* **Bottle and glass** – *arse*. The original rhyme that birthed another piece of slang – *Aristotle* (to rhyme with 'bottle'). This was then shortened to *arris*, which is now in widespread use by many who are no longer aware of its rhyming origins. The equally well-known alternative is *Khyber Pass*, after a mountain pass in the Hindu Kush range connecting Afghanistan and Pakistan, which played a pivotal role in British imperial history. Its slang usage might also be a wry nod to the potential effects of the region's traditional spicy food. A more modern variant is *Myleene Klass*, after the reality TV pop star, classical superstar and popular television host. No doubt her place

in slang culture was boosted by her appearance on *I'm a Celebrity . . . Get Me Out of Here!*, during which she famously showered in a teeny-tiny bikini.

* **Clothes pegs** – *legs*. Alternatives are *hams and eggs*, *scotch eggs* and *scotch pegs*.

* **Eyes front** – *cunt*. A rhyme derived from the military. Also *growl and grunt*, seemingly incorporating an allusion to the sounds of sexual intercourse. In recent years the rhyme has been adapted to *growler*.

* **Fox and badger** – *tadger*. Tadger is a term for the penis which has been used in the north of England for several centuries.

* **Gary Glitter** – *shitter*. A particularly graphic slang term coined in an age before the Glam Rock star was convicted of a series of paedophile offences.

* **Glue pot** – *twat* (pronounced here as 'twot'). Sometimes replaced by *mustard pot*, which probably stems from the Victorian slang *mustard and cress* for pubic hair.

* **Gobstopper** – *chopper*. With pretty crude connotations of fellatio.

* **Grandfather clock** – *cock*. A classic phallic symbol presumably used by gents with a particularly high opinion of themselves. Also used is *Blackpool rock*, referencing one of George Formby's most popular songs and its innuendo-laden lyrics: 'With my little stick of Blackpool Rock, along the promenade I stroll, / In my pocket it got stuck I could

tell / 'Cos when I pulled it out I pulled my shirt off as well.'

* **Hampton Wick** – *prick* (or alternatively, *dick*). Hampton Wick is a genteel neighbourhood in south-west London. Its use as slang for the male member is perhaps a sly attack on its image of middle-class correctness. It has also spurred the sub-rhyme *Lionel Hampton*, after the great American jazz musician. Thus slang speakers may refer to a *Hampton* or a *Lionel*.

* **Jacob's Cream Crackers** – *knackers* (as in 'testicles'). In which that staple of the tea table, the dry biscuit to accompany cheese, is hijacked.

* **Leslie Ash** – *gash*. Ash was the focus of much male attention when she played the desirable next-door-neighbour in the 1990s sitcom *Men Behaving Badly*, that era's classic acclamation of juvenile masculinity. The word *gash* used in the context of the female genitals can be traced back to the eighteenth century.

* **London taxi** – *jacksie*. Jacksie has been in popular use as a term for the buttocks since the nineteenth century.

* **Mars and Venus** – *penis*. A rhyme that utilizes the Roman gods representative of the difference between the sexes.

* **Orchestra stalls** – *balls* (as in 'testicles'). Thematically, it is but a small jump to *Henry Halls*, a nod to Henry Hall, the south London-born leader of the BBC Dance Orchestra from the 1930s who became a household name. *Max Walls* is also used. Max Wall was born in Brixton in 1908 and

developed from a music hall favourite into one of the greats of British comedy, as well as winning accolades for straight acting roles in older age.

* **Plates of meat** – *feet*. One of the best known of all rhyming slang phrases. A less common, and even less appealing, alternative is *dog's meat*.

* **Sandra Bullocks** – *bollocks*. A lasting and not entirely inventive monument to the queen of the modern Hollywood comedy.

* **Seb Coes** – *toes*. Paying homage to Sebastian Coe, one of Britain's greatest ever middle-distance runners known for his devastating acceleration towards the end of races. The rhyme is used particularly in the sense of 'having it away on your sebs' (i.e. to make a quick escape).

* **Sigourney Weaver** – *beaver*. Taking advantage of the film star's name to make a rhyme with the American slang term for the female genitalia.

* **Uncle Bob** – *knob*. A rhyme masterful in its simplicity and relative innocence.

SLANG IN ACTION

They were an odd couple, Cindy and Fred. She was 22, he was 85. She had a lovely blonde *barnet*. He was *cyril*. She had beautiful *minces* and a little, turned-up *ruby*. He had sticky-out *tobys* and a massive *pea-shooter*. She had plump *apples* and he had false *hampsteads*. She had *cabman's rests* out to there and *scotch pegs* up to here. He had a *limehouse* out to there and *scotch pegs* that only just touched the ground. But they were happy. Till his *strawberry* gave out.

Translation

They were an odd couple, Cindy and Fred. She was 22, he was 85. She had lovely blonde *hair*. He was *bald*. She had beautiful *eyes* and a little, turned-up *nose*. He had sticky-out *ears* and a massive *hooter*. She had plump *lips* and he had false *teeth*. She had *breasts* out to there and *legs* up to here. He had a *gut* out to there and *legs* that only just touched the ground. But they were happy. Till his *heart* gave out.

—m—

VISITING MY AUNT'S: BODILY FUNCTIONS

Visiting my aunt's – *Going to the lavatory*. *My Aunt's* is slang for
Mrs Chant's. Mrs Chant was Ormiston Chant (1848–1923), a noted
feminist, social reformer and occasional prude. 'Visiting Mrs Chant's'
became a euphemistic way of saying you were going to the lavatory.

—∾—

Here is a selection of phrases used to talk about unmentionable
things.

* **Andy Capp** – *crap*. Capp is the flat cap-wearing, working-
  class eponymous hero of the comic strip created by Reg
  Smythe which has appeared in the *Daily Mirror* and
  Sunday Mirror since 1957.

* **Cat and dog** – *bog*. Also sometimes *Kermit the Frog*.

* **Cuddle and kiss** – *piss*. A rather strange choice of rhyme.
  Alternatives, equally unedifying, include *gypsy's kiss*, *French
  kiss* and *goodnight kiss*. Also in use is *snake's hiss*, which at
  least has some onomatopoeic quality while snake can be
  employed euphemistically in reference to the male
  member (as in 'trouser snake').

* **Cup of tea** – *pee*. A neat rhyme connecting cause and effect.

* **Jenny Lind** – *wind*. Jenny Lind was a nineteenth-century opera star, nicknamed 'the Swedish Nightingale', who boasted remarkable lung capacity.

* **Jimmy Logie** – *bogie*. Jimmy Logie was Arsenal's Scottish international centre forward from 1939 to 1955, winning two League titles and the FA Cup.

* **Jimmy Riddle** – *piddle*. One of the most widely known of all slang terms. Whether there was ever a real Jimmy Riddle behind it is unclear.

* **Johnny Cash** – *slash* (as in 'urinate'). After the legendary American country and western singer.

* **Rag and bone** – *throne* (another euphemistic term for a toilet). Rag and bone men were once common sights in London, recycling old rags and bones (the latter of which could be turned into, for instance, glue) for personal profit. There is perhaps some sense of both the slang and its corresponding subject being receptacles for waste.

* **Raquel Welch** – *belch*. Welch is a buxom American actress known for roles in films such as *One Million Years BC*.

* **Raspberry tart** – *fart*. A rhyme that plays on the alternative meaning of raspberry as the act of sticking your tongue between your lips and blowing out to create a sound reminiscent of passing wind. An alternative is *D'Oyly Carte*, referring to the opera company most famous for producing

Steptoe and Son

Steptoe and Son is regarded as one of the greatest sitcoms of all time. Written by Alan Simpson and Ray Galton, it ran from 1962 until 1974, following the ups and downs of the titular father and son as they ran their rag and bone business in Shepherd's Bush. The use of rhyming slang was frequent and the programme exposed itself to earthy language of a sort not often heard on the BBC in that era. In one episode, for instance, the son Harold (played by Harry H. Corbett) told his father, Albert (Wilfrid Brambell): "If you feel like a d'Oyly Carte [*fart*], you go outside."

the works of Gilbert and Sullivan. The rhyme thus boyishly suggests a musicality to breaking wind.

* **Richard the Third** – *turd*. Richard is sometimes replaced by *George*. A perhaps overly graphic alternative is *lemon curd*.

* **Rosie O'Grady's** – *ladies* (as in 'toilets'). 'Sweet Rosie O'Grady' was a sentimental ballad written by Maude Nugent and published in 1896.

* **Savoury rissole** – *pisshole*. A reasonably modern and rather laboured addition to the lexicon.

* **Tomtit** – *shit*. A phrase given new life by Jim Royle, head of TV's *Royle Family*, who would often announce, newspaper under arm, that he was going off for a 'tomtit'. A tomtit is in literal terms a small bird.

* **Wallace and Gromit** – *vomit*. Wallace is the animated inventor and cheese fanatic created by Nick Park and his Aardman Animations team, while Gromit is his trusty dog. Regulars at the Oscars, their usage here raises the question, 'Too much Wensleydale, Wallace?'

* **Wyatt Earp** – *burp*. Earp is one of the legendary figures of the Wild West. Along with his brothers, Virgil and Morgan, plus 'Doc' Holliday, he was a participant in the gunfight at the O.K. Corral in 1881.

* **Zorba the Greek** – *leak* (as in 'urinate'). *Zorba the Greek* was a novel by Nikos Kazantzakis published in 1946 and brought to the silver screen in 1964.

SLANG IN ACTION

I needed a *cuddle* so I asked the barman where the *cat* was. He said the gents was out of order, but I could pop into the *rosie* if I was quick. As I was having a *jimmy*, I heard some woman stroll in. As she touched up her lippy she gave out the loudest *raquel* I've ever heard. When I'd finished and was washing my hands, I said, 'Not very ladylike.' She looked me up and down and said, 'You're one to talk.'

Translation

I needed a *piss* so I asked the barman where the *bog* was. He said the gents was out of order, but I could pop into the *ladies* if I was quick. As I was having a *piddle*, I heard some woman stroll in. As she touched up her lippy she gave out the loudest *belch* I've ever heard. When I'd finished and was washing my hands, I said, 'Not very ladylike.' She looked me up and down and said, 'You're one to talk.'

—ɯ—

SHILLINGS AND PENCE: THE MIND AND THE SENSES

Shillings and pence – *Sense*. A rhyme implying the dubious notion that wealth is an indicator of intelligence.

—※—

A section dealing with vocabulary related not only to the mind and its improvement but to the human senses in general.

NOW AND NEVER – Clever

A miscellany of words to do with the brain and how to keep it occupied and healthy. All in the interests of keeping you from going *Mum and Dad* (*mad*; suggestive of the eccentricities one can witness within the confines of the domestic setting).

* **Bo Peep** – *sleep*. Referencing the nursery rhyme about the neglectful shepherdess, including the lines:
  'Little Bo-peep fell fast asleep, / And dreamt she heard them bleating.'

* **Earwig** – *twig* (as in 'to understand').

* **Feather and flip** – *kip* (as in sleep). A phrase that brings to mind not only downy pillows but the tossing and turning of the sleeper.

* **Lion's roar** – *snore*. As anyone forced to sleep near a snorer will know, a most appropriate rhyme. Similarly, the alternative *rain and pour*.

Literacy

* **Bill and Ben** – *pen*. The rhyme references the Flower Pot Men, two of the most popular characters to appear on children's TV since they debuted in 1952. They converse in the made-up language of Oddle Poddle and have notably little use of pens.

* **Dicky bird** – *word*. A rhyme of the 1930s that recalls the phrase, 'A little bird told me'.

* **Rookery Nook** – *book*. *Rookery Nook* is, suitably enough, the title of a 1923 book by Ben Travers. An alternative rhyme is *Captain Cook* after James Cook, the legendary English explorer.

* **Skyscraper** – *newspaper*. A rhyme that evokes the image of a newspaper office in Manhattan, *à la* Clark Kent and the *Daily Planet*. An alternative rhyme from a slightly earlier era is *linen draper*.

Charles Dickens

No other writer gets as many mentions in this survey of rhyming slang as Charles Dickens, whose own name and those of several of his literary characters have been picked up by rhymers. Born in 1812, he spent the greater part of his life in London and much of his literary output investigates its injustices and inequalities. His father spent a period of time in the notorious Marshalsea prison for debtors in Southwark, while Charles worked in a law office and as a reporter, which helped increase his knowledge of the city's darker side.

For all that, there is an almost curious absence of rhyming slang in his novels. Although this slang was firmly established by the time that *A Tale of Two Cities* was published in 1859, its most notable Cockney, Jerry Cruncher, makes no use of it. When Dickens wrote an essay on slang for the weekly journal *Household Words* in September 1853, he did not acknowledge the existence of rhyming slang. His words, though, suggest that he would not have been much in favour: 'I must express my opinion either that slang should be proscribed, banished, prohibited, or that a New Dictionary should be compiled, in which all the slang terms now in use among educated men ... should be registered, etymologised, explained, and stamped with the lexicographic stamp ... If the evil of slang has grown too gigantic to be suppressed, let us at least give it decency by legalising it.'

Numeracy

* **Penny bun** – *one*. Dating from the beginning of the twentieth century when one could still buy a cake and get change out of tuppence.

* **Me and you** – *two*. A simple piece of arithmetic.

* **Vicar of Bray** – *trey* (an antiquated word for three). The vicar in question was Simon Aleyn, the parish priest for Bray in Berkshire who reputedly vacillated between Protestantism and Roman Catholicism in order to remain in his post during the religious upheavals of the sixteenth century.

* **Knock on the door** – *four*.

* **Beehive** – *five*.

* **Chopsticks** – *six*.

* **God in heaven** – *seven*. An alternative rhyme is *gates of heaven*.

* **Garden gate** – *eight*.

* **Mother of mine** – *nine*. Further evidence that the family (and especially Mum) is never far from a slang-speaker's mind.

* **Big Ben** – *ten*. After the giant bell in the Clock Tower of the Houses of Parliament.

* **Horn of Plenty** – *twenty*.

119

* **Pompey whore** – *twenty-four*. Pompey is the nickname
  of Portsmouth, the naval town on England's south coast.
  In common with other places boasting docks and large
  numbers of seamen, it garnered quite a reputation for
  prostitution.

University Degrees

Reflecting an age when unprecedented numbers of people have
had access to higher education, slang-speakers have conjured up
rhymes to denote certain classifications of university degree.

* **Geoff Hurst** – *First*. After the striker who played for West
  Ham and scored a hat-trick for England against West
  Germany in the 1966 World Cup final – the first, and thus
  far only, player to achieve the feat in the sport's most
  important game.
* **Attila** – *Two-one*. After Attila the Hun, the fifth-century
  rampaging leader of the Huns not principally renowned
  for his studies.
* **Desmond** – *Two-two*. After Desmond Tutu, the Nobel
  Peace Prize-winning Archbishop of Cape Town who
  played an instrumental role in bringing an end to
  apartheid in South Africa and oversaw its Truth and
  Reconciliation Commission.
* **Douglas Hurd** – *Third*. After the former Conservative
  Foreign Secretary who, incidentally, came third in his

party's leadership contest in 1990 (and in his youth earned a First in History from Cambridge). Alternatively *George* or *Richard the Third*

THE SENSES

* **Anna May Wong** – *pong*. After the first female Asian-American to make it in the movies, winning fame in the 1920s in *The Toll of the Sea* and *The Thief of Baghdad*.

* **Bacon rind** – *blind*. Pigs are considered to generally have poor eyesight.

* **Butcher's hook** – *look*. One of the phrases everyone knows, dating from the nineteenth century, referring to the double-ended hook employed by butchers when hanging meat.

* **Errol Flynns** – *bins* (short for binoculars and here understood as spectacles). Flynn was Australian by birth and the greatest screen swashbuckler that ever lived. His movies included *Captain Blood* (1935), and *The Adventures of Robin Hood* (1938).

* **Girls and boys** – *noise*. One of those rhymes that encapsulates cause and effect.

* **Judi Dench** – *stench*. A wholly inappropriate rhyme for the fragrant grande dame of British acting.

* **Mountain passes** – *glasses*. An alternative is *working classes*.

* **Mutt and Jeff** – *deaf*. Mutt and Jeff were the stars of an American comic strip that appeared for the first time around 1907 and continued until the 1980s. Augustus Mutt was a none-too-bright horse racing addict while Jeff was a former inmate of an insane asylum and had a similar passion. The rhyme is often contracted to 'mutton'.

* **Pen and ink** – *stink*. A mid-Victorian rhyme.

* **Pipe your eye** – *cry*. A remarkably illustrative rhyme.

* **William Tell** – *smell*. After the Swiss folk hero of the fourteenth century who famously had enough faith in his skills with the crossbow to shoot an apple off his son's head. An alternative rhyme is *heaven and hell*, suggestive of the contrasting effects different smells can have on the olfactory sense.

SLANG IN ACTION

Trevor is *now and never*. At school, all the teachers were impressed with how quick he was to *earwig*. He eats lots of fish, drinks water by the gallon and has plenty of *feather* to keep his brain lively. He has a way with *dickys*, his head is always in a *rookery* and he got a *geoff* at university. But he's blind as a bat and has lost his *mountains*. They're perched on the top of his head. *Now and never* but no *shillings*!

Translation

Trevor is *clever*. At school, all the teachers were impressed with how quick he was to *twig*. He eats lots of fish, drinks water by the gallon and has plenty of *kip* to keep his brain lively. He has a way with *words*, his head is always in a *book* and he got a *first* at university. But he's blind as a bat and has lost his *glasses*. They're perched on the top of his head. *Clever* but no *sense*!

—⧖—

TOM AND DICK: HEALTH

Tom and Dick – *Sick*. A pared-down version of 'Tom, Dick and Harry', the term used as shorthand for a group of nondescript individuals.

—∾—

Ill health can include embarrassing symptoms, so confidentiality is often desirable. In such circumstances, rhyming slang comes into its own, though some of these phrases might leave your doctor a little bewildered …

* **Basil Brush** – *thrush*. Basil Brush is a debonair fox glove-puppet who has entertained generations of kids since the 1960s with his bad jokes and catchphrase of 'Boom! Boom!'

* **Beattie and Babs** – *crabs* (pubic lice). Beattie and Babs were a popular double act on the music hall scene in the early decades of the twentieth century.

* **Bread and cheese** – *sneeze*. A rhyme from the nineteenth century to put you off your tea.

* **Cape Horns** – *corns*. Cape Horn is the southernmost tip of South America.

* **Chalfont St Giles** – *piles*. A cheeky rhyme at the expense of a notably genteel village in Buckinghamshire. *Johnny Giles* is also used by some, after the Irish football international who enjoyed great success as an abundantly skilled midfielder. Similarly unfortunately monikered is *Annabel Giles*, the model, broadcaster and former wife of Midge Ure.

* **Conan Doyle** – *boil*. Not only was Conan Doyle the creator of the greatest crime-fighting duo in history, Sherlock Holmes and Doctor Watson, he himself was a medical doctor.

* **Cream-crackered** – *knackered*. Cream crackers are the perfect postprandial accompaniment to a good, strong cheese – a tradition much beloved of the British.

* **East India Docks** – *pox*. The East India Docks, built in the early nineteenth century, were situated in Blackwall, close to the Isle of Dogs, and might justifiably claim to be one of the spiritual homes of Cockney rhyming slang.. Alternatively, rhymers might use *Tilbury Docks*, another of the Thames's most important port complexes, opened in 1886 and located in Essex.

* **Emma Freuds** – *haemorrhoids*. Daughter of broadcaster Clement, sister of PR guru Matthew, niece of painter Lucien and great-granddaughter of psychoanalyst Sigmund, Emma Freud hails from a famous dynasty. She

has regularly appeared on television and radio and works as a script adviser on the works of her partner, Richard Curtis.

* **Eartha Kitts** – *the shits* (as in diarrhoea). An unfortunate rhyme that references Kitt, the great American singer and actress (1927–2008). On her death *The Times* described her as 'the original pussy cat doll'.

* **Fanny Hills** – *pills*. Fanny Hill is the subject of John Cleland's long-banned 1748 novel, *Memoirs of a Woman of Pleasure*, arguably English literature's first pornographic novel.

* **Frock and frill** – *chill*. Dating from the late Victorian age and evoking the female clothing of that time.

* **Hangar Lane** – *pain*. One of the most notorious stretches of London's North Circular Road. Regularly the scene of nightmarish tailbacks.

* **Harold Pinter** – *splinter*. Pinter, who died in 2008, was one of the shining lights of the theatre scene from the moment his second play, *The Birthday Party*, wowed audiences in 1958. You might want to insert a long pause before coming out with this particular rhyme.

* **Horse and trap** – *the clap* (as in gonorrhoea). Often used in the context of generalized sexually transmitted diseases.

* **Horse and trough** – *cough*. Offering a neat pun on 'hoarse'.

* **Inky blue** – *flu*. A rhyme that describes the mood that the illness can bring on.

* **Life and death** – *breath*. Giving due recognition to the most basic of life's processes.

* **Little Tich** – *itch*. Little Tich was the stage name of Harry Relph (1867–1928), a star of the London vaudeville scene. He stopped growing at four foot six, and his most famous act involved him prancing around in twenty-eight-inch boots.

* **Lord Sutch** – *crutch*. David Sutch (1940–99) was better known as Screaming Lord Sutch, founder and leader of the Official Monster Raving Loony Party. After embarking on a best-forgotten music career in the 1960s, he founded his political party in 1983 and contested numerous elections, none of which he ever won. On one occasion he was invited to take tea on the House of Commons terrace. On his arrival he hung a plank of wood, complete with drawers, around the neck of an MP and declared, 'Let's have a cabinet meeting'. He was generally considered to have brightened up British politics.

* **Naughton and Gold** – *cold*. The rhyme references Charlie Naughton and Jimmy Gold, a comedy double act whose career stretched across seven decades, working for much of that time as part of the legendary Crazy Gang.

* **Nellie Duff** – *puff*. Not modelled on any real person. And what you don't want to run out of!

* **Petticoat Lane** – *pain*. One of the most famous of all London markets, with a history going back to at least the

Tudor period. Located east of the City, it has, as its name suggests, a particular reputation for clothing.

* **Radio Ones** – *the runs* (as in diarrhoea). Radio 1, the BBC's leading pop music radio station, has down the years employed many disc jockeys who have suffered from acute verbal diarrhoea. An alternative expression is *Tommy guns* (short for the Thompson sub-machine gun), particularly associated with Prohibition gangsters like Al Capone. It was renowned for its rapid fire, which may be partly responsible for its adoption in this context.

* **Randolph Scotts** – *spots*. Scott was an American actor who started out as a comedy lead in the 1930s but became best known for gritty Westerns from the 1940s to the 1960s.

* **Rising damp** – *cramp*. Conjures up a pleasing analogy between the spread of damp and the spread of pain.

* **Spanish onion** – *bunion*. A wonderfully graphic rhyme for the unpleasant foot complaint. Medical science suggests that onions do indeed have some anti-inflammatory properties so they might even help counter the condition.

* **Ugly Sister** – *blister*. The Ugly Sisters are a pantomime staple, the revolting siblings of Cinderella. A suitable rhyme for such an unpleasant subject.

SLANG IN ACTION

Harry went to the doctor's. He'd not been feeling well for a while. It began with a *bread* and a *horse* so he though he had a *naughton*. Then he got the *hangars* and a *frock* and felt completely *cream-crackered*, so he thought it was *inky blue*. The doctor prescribed him some plasters and some pills. 'What are these for?' Harry asked. 'Those are for *cape horns*, that's for *chalfonts* and those are for *beatties*,' said the doctor. He has since been struck off.

Translation

Harry went to the doctor's. He'd not been feeling well for a while. It began with a *sneeze* and a *cough* so he though he had a *cold*. Then he got the *pains* and a *chill* and felt completely *knackered*, so he thought it was *flu*. The doctor prescribed him some plasters and some pills. 'What are these for?' Harry asked. 'Those are for *corns*, that's for *piles* and those are for *crabs*,' said the doctor. He has since been struck off.

—ᴍ—

OEDIPUS REX: SEX

Oedipus Rex – Sex. Sophocles' tragedy *Oedipus Rex* was first performed around 429 BC. The story sees Oedipus kill his father, Laius, and marry his mother, Jocasta – casting Oedipus as the epitomy of sexual confusion for evermore. Another rhyme for *sex* is *T. Rex*, after the great glam rock band of the 1970s, whose lead singer Marc Bolan occupied the thoughts of many a lustful teen.

—⁂—

As you might expect, the slang in this chapter has not been designed to save anybody's blushes.

* **Aylesbury duck** – *fuck*. Aylesbury ducks come from Buckinghamshire and are prized historically for their good eating. Beatrix Potter's Jemima Puddle-Duck was an example of the breed. An alternative from the early twentieth century is *trolley and truck*.

* **Brass nail** – *tail* (as in 'prostitute'). Usually contracted to 'brass' and given widespread exposure in any number of gritty TV cop dramas.

* **Flake of corn** – *horn* (i.e. erection). An alternative is *early morn*.

* **Flying sixty-six** – *French tricks* (that is to say 'oral sex'). As so often, the English implicate the French in acts of lasciviousness. The proximity of sixty-six to sixty-nine (the nickname given to the act of mutual oral stimulation) is probably no coincidence.

* **General election** – *erection*. Members standing? Exit polls? Feel free to make your own jokes.

* **Herring and kipper** – *stripper*. One of rhyming slang's least appealing phrases.

* **Hit and miss** – *kiss*. Any dalliance is likely to begin with one of these and the rhyme emphasizes the 'pot luck' strategy adopted by many in search of companionship.

* **J. Arthur Rank** – *wank*. As the founder of the Rank Organisation, J. Arthur was one of the great figures of British cinema, responsible for such classics as *The Red Shoes*, *Black Narcissus* and Olivier's *Henry V*, and was involved with a number of the *Carry On* films. One of the stars of that series, Kenneth Williams, favoured the rhyme *Barclays Bank*. Another alternative is *Sherman tank*, the principal tank used by US forces during the Second World War and replete with obvious phallic symbolism.

* **Jane Shore** – *whore*. Shore was a noted beauty and courtesan who lived from *c.* 1445 to 1527 and whose list

of paramours included Edward IV, who described her as 'the merriest harlot'. Alternatively, *bolt the door* might be used (the phrase usually adapted to 'old bolt').

* **John Bull** – *pull* (as in 'going on the pull'). Sex in the city very often begins in such a way. John Bull, traditionally depicted as a portly figure in a bowler hat and Union Jack waistcoat, may not be the archetype of sex appeal, but he is nonetheless the personification of English manhood.

* **Lover's tiff** – *syphilis*. A rather coy rhyme for a sexually transmitted disease which, in some cases, can prove fatal.

* **Maria Monk** – *spunk* (as in 'semen'). Monk was a Canadian nun who claimed to have been sexually exploited at a Montreal convent where illicit liaisons with priests and infanticide were commonplace. Updating the rhyme a little, the jazz great *Thelonius Monk* has had the misfortune of being taken up by some slang-speakers.

* **Me and you** – *screw* (as in 'fornicate'). A relatively tamer rhyme that, with the addition of a question mark, might serve as a hopeful chat-up line.

* **Melvyn Bragg** – *shag*. A reference to the tousled-haired man of the arts and one of Britain's premier broadcasters.

* **Mix and muddle** – *cuddle*. A phrase highlighting the potential awkwardness of the embrace.

* **Pass in the pot** – *hot* (as in 'sexy'). Dating from the nineteenth century, when for the sake of decency 'pass' was used instead of 'piss'. Such delicacy seems misplaced considering much of the other slang in this section.

* **Plate of ham** – *gam* (as in 'fellatio'). A grimly graphic image, 'gam' being a mid-nineteenth-century word with French origins used by prostitutes for this sex act.

* **Port and brandy** – *randy*. Though no longer the drink of choice of young men out on the John Bull, the rhyme draws a clear link between alcohol and heightened desire.

* **Reggie and Ronnie** – *condom*. Not rhyming but exquisitely Cockney slang. It refers to the Kray twins, among whose many business interests was the provision of 'protection' throughout the East End.

* **Roberta Flack** – *sack* (as in 'I want to get her in the sack'). Flack is one of the most soulful singers of contemporary American music whose hits include, appropriately, 'Feel Like Makin' Love'.

* **Uriah Heep** – *creep*. What any young male looking for love should aim not to be. Heep was the ginger-haired, cadaverous and utterly cloying office clerk in Charles Dickens's *David Copperfield*. His repulsive and self-serving obsequiousness ensures that this is one of the most appropriate phrases in all rhyming slang.

SLANG IN ACTION

Lee and Nigel were out on a night on the *john*. They ended up in some dodgy club full of *herrings*. But there was one girl at the bar that caught Nigel's eye and he was determined to get her into the *roberta*. He brought her a couple of drinks and was feeling very *port*. He was about to move in for a *hit* and *mix* and meant to whisper a sweet nothing in her ear. He said, 'Fancy a *melvyn*?' instead. She looked him in the eye and said, 'Not with you, *Uriah*.'

Translation

Lee and Nigel were out on a night on the *pull*. They ended up in some dodgy club full of *strippers*. But there was one girl at the bar that caught Nigel's eye and he was determined to get her into the *sack*. He brought her a couple of drinks and was feeling very *randy*. He was about to move in for a *kiss* and *cuddle* and meant to whisper a sweet nothing in her ear. He said, 'Fancy a *shag*?' instead. She looked him in the eye and said, 'Not with you, *creep*.'

—∿—

HARRY LIME, DRUM AND BASS, HAT AND FEATHER: TIME, PLACE AND WEATHER

This chapter deals with slang terms for time, place and weather. There are several references to the great British climate, for example *blue and grey* (day) and *Aunt Ella* (*umbrella*).

HARRY LIME – Time

After the anti-hero of *The Third Man*, the classic film noir with a screenplay by Graham Greene. Lime, an amoral black marketeer, was played by Orson Welles and famously declared on the subject of time: 'In Switzerland, they had brotherly love, they had five hundred years of democracy and peace – and what did that produce? The cuckoo clock.'

—⚏—

* **Alligator** – *later*. Stemming from the lyrics of the song 'See You Later Alligator', written by Bobby Charles and released by Bill Haley & His Comets in 1956.

* **Black and white** – *night*. An inevitable rhyme given the association between night and blackness.

135

* **Blue and grey** – *day*. A rhyme evoking a picture of the classic British sky.

* **Bubble and squeak** – *week*. Based on a staple of the cooked full English breakfast consisting of fried potatoes and green vegetables.

* **Cock linnet** – *minute*. The linnet is a member of the finch family kept as pets in great number in the Victorian and Edwardian eras. In Fred W. Leigh and Charles Collins's music hall classic *My Old Man*, for a long while a pillar of Marie Lloyd's act, the narrator sings: 'My old man said 'Follow the van, / And don't dilly dally on the way'. / Off went the van wiv me 'ome packed in it, / I followed on wiv me old cock linnet.'

* **Dickory-dock** – *clock*. Referencing the nursery rhyme (in circulation since at least the mid-eighteenth century) that runs: 'Hickory, dickory, dock / The mouse ran up the clock.'

* **Gordon and Gotch** – *watch*. The rhyme relates to a long-defunct book distribution company that was based in Plaistow, east London.

* **Gypsy's warning** – *morning*. The rhyme may derive from the song *The Gypsy's Warning*, written in 1864, about a young woman being warned off the attentions of an untrustworthy male. It includes the lyrics: 'Now thy life is in its morning / Cloud not this thy happy lot. / Listen to the gypsy's warning, gentle lady, / Heed him not.' A rather quainter mid-Victorian alternative was *maids adorning*.

136

* **Harry Tate** – *late*. After the music hall performer and film actor (1872–1940) who ditched his real surname, Hutchinson, for a stage name taken from one of his previous employers, the sugar magnate Henry Tate.

DRUM AND BASS – Place

After a form of bass-heavy, breakbeat dance music popular in the 1990s.

—ⱳ—

* **Coffee and tea** – *sea*. A rhyme comparing vastly different liquids.

* **Field of wheat** – *street*. Bringing to mind that timeless observation of the nostalgic: 'I remember when it was all fields around here.' Also used is *Postman's Knock*, a game in which players kiss each other.

* **Jack and Jill** – *hill*. Recalling the nursery rhyme with the lines 'Jack and Jill went up the hill / To fetch a pail of water.'

* **Joan of Arc** – *park*. After the saintly Maid of Orléans, who led French armies against the English during the Hundred Years War and was eventually captured and burnt at the stake.

* **Mother Brown** – *town*. Referencing the 1938 hit by Weston and Lee about the lady who loved a good knees-up, a song played at many an East End party.

* **Old Oak** – *Big Smoke* (as in 'London'). The capital garnered the nickname 'Big Smoke' (and sometimes just 'the Smoke') because of the vast amounts of smoke (and other fumes) pumped out there. The rhyme evokes one of the great symbols of England and brings to mind the naval march 'Heart of Oak', suggesting London as the heart of the nation.

* **Safe and sound** – *the ground*. A rhyme perhaps coined by a landlubber and disciple of the creed of terra firma.

* **Shake and shiver** – *river*. The rhyme is indicative of how you might feel after a dunk in the water.

ANIMALS

* **Ball of fat** – *cat*. Drawing a picture of an over-pampered feline.

* **Bo Peep** – *sheep*. Referencing the shepherdess of nursery rhyme fame, who lacked basic skills in keeping her flock together.

* **Charing Cross** – *horse*. A mid-nineteenth-century rhyme when London dialects allowed 'cross' and 'horse' to rhyme more closely than they do today. Charing Cross has long been considered the centre point of the city and thus a major transport hub. In days gone by that meant huge numbers of horses were seen in the area.

* **Cherry Hog** – *dog*. A cherry hog is an antiquated phrase denoting a cherry stone. An alternative is *London fog*. The worst fogs the capital experienced were during the nineteenth and early twentieth centuries, when burning soft coal led to pea-soupers.

* **Jerusalem artichoke** – *moke* (a nineteenth-century term for a donkey). The allusion to Jersualem brings to mind Christ's entry into that city on an ass.

* **Lord Wigg** – *pig*. Lord Wigg was the Labour politician George Wigg (1900–83) who served as the eyes and ears for Prime Minister Harold Wilson within the Labour Party. Thus there may be the idea of a 'squealer' behind the rhyme.

RODENTS, BIRDS AND INSECTS

* **Bow and arrow** – *sparrow*. Creating an association between two objects that fly through the air.

* **Maxwell House** – *mouse*. Referring to a popular brand of instant coffee.

* **Nice one, Cyril** – *squirrel*. From a 1972 television advert for Wonderloaf, which culminated in a baker called Cyril being congratulated on his wares. Fans of Tottenham Hotspur Football Club adapted it to praise their left back, Cyril Knowles. The Cockerel Chorus had a top twenty hit in March 1973 with a song containing the refrain, 'Nice one, Cyril, nice one, son / Nice one, Cyril, let's 'ave another one'.

* **Meat pie** – *fly*. Suggestive of a pie shop with unfavourable hygiene standards.

* **Richard the Third** – *bird*. The much-reviled king, held responsible by many for the deaths of the little princes, Edward and Richard, in the Tower of London in 1483, is perhaps more commonly used as a rhyme for *turd*.

* **Sit beside her** – *spider*. A nursery rhyme reference to Little Miss Muffet, who abandoned not only her tuffet but her curds and whey as well when an arachnid did, indeed, 'sit beside her'.

* **Stand at ease** – *fleas*. A play on the military command wholly inappropriate for someone beset with the little beasts.

HAT AND FEATHER – Weather

A rhyme suggestive of ways to keep yourself snug in an adverse climate.

—⚏—

* **Aunt Ella** – *umbrella*. Not believed to be based on any real person. Rihanna, however, inadvertently gives her a name check in her 2007 smash hit, 'Umbrella', which has a chorus of: 'You can stand under my umbrella / (Ella ella eh eh eh).'

* **Bath bun** – *sun*. Referring to the traditional sweetened cake closely associated with the West Country city.

* **Buck and doe** – *snow*. A rhyme that sounds abruptly rude when delivered with a Cockney lilt.

* **France and Spain** – *rain*. A rhyme that chimes with the famous elocution exercise from *My Fair Lady*: 'The rain in Spain stays mainly on the plain.'

* **Eiffel Tower** – *shower*. A logical progression from the rhyme above to one of the most familiar symbols of France.

* **Night and day** – *grey*. An apposite rhyme if one considers night to signify darkness and day to signify light.

* **Peas in the pot** – *hot*. Conjuring up an image of a saucepan simmering away on the hob.

* **Potatoes in the mould** – *cold*. Here 'mould' refers to the ground, conjuring up an image of a frosty veg patch.

* **Rawalpindi** – *windy*. An exotic reference to the city now in the Punjab province of Pakistan and formerly in India when the country was still part of the British Empire. In that period it was the largest British military garrison in the Raj.

* **Shepherd's pie** – *sky*. There has long been an association between shepherds and the sky through folkloric weather forecasts such as 'Red sky at night; shepherds delight' and 'Red sky in the morning; shepherds warning'.

* **Silver spoon** – *moon*. Drawing on an obvious correlation between the bowl of a spoon and a full moon.

* **Soldiers bold** – *cold*. Dating from the nineteenth century.

* **Stand from under** – *thunder*. A phrase shouted to encourage someone to move out of the way of a falling object, as here in Mark Twain's *The Adventures of Huckleberry Finn*: 'there warn't nothing to do but just hold still, and try and be ready to stand from under when the lightning struck.'

* **Uncle Willie** – *chilly*. Not based on any known uncle.

The Two Ronnies

Ronnie Barker and Ronnie Corbett together formed The Two Ronnies, one of the most popular comedy acts of all time. Many of their sketches revelled in complex wordplay and in one particularly memorable sketch Barker is a vicar delivering his sermon in rhyming slang. It made much of the audience's familiarity with the slang *Richard the Third*, correctly assuming that most people would immediately think of its cruder association. The sketch finishes 'and he bent down and picked up that long, brown Richard the Third and placed it on a wall ... and soon afterwards, that long brown Richard the Third flew off to its nest.'

SLANG IN ACTION

After I'd gone into *mother brown*, I walked home via the *joan*. It knocked a couple of *cocks* off the journey, see. Only while I was there a *bow* dived at me from out of the *shepherd*. I put my hands up to protect myself and that's when I think my *gordon* must have fallen off my wrist and on to the *safe*. So now I don't know what *harry* it is and when I wake up, the *gypsys* are so dark that I'm not even sure if it's *black* or *blue*.

Translation

After I'd gone into *town*, I walked home via the *park*. It knocked a couple of *minutes* off the journey, see. Only while I was there a *sparrow* dived at me from out of the *sky*. I put my hands up to protect myself and that's when I think my *watch* must have fallen off my wrist and on to the *ground*. So now I don't know what *time* it is and when I wake up, the *mornings* are so dark that I'm not even sure if it's *night* or *day*.

—◦◦◦—

THE FROG AND TOAD:
TRANSPORT AND TRAVEL

The frog and toad – *the road*. A mid-nineteenth-century phrase reflecting the novelty of seeing amphibious life that most Londoners only ever experienced when travelling away from the city.

—⚡—

Though your true Cockney never feels the need to stray too far beyond the sound of Bow Bells, inevitably there are times when they have to hit the old *frog*.

* **Ball of chalk** – *walk*.

* **Bat and wicket** – *ticket*. A rhyme with a cricketing heritage.

* **Billy Liar** – *tyre*. References the eponymous (anti-)hero of Keith Waterhouse's 1959 novel, in which William Fisher tries to imagine himself out of his life as an undertaker's clerk in Yorkshire but struggles to shackle his lying.

* **Camilla Parker Bowles** – *Rolls-Royce*. Honouring the wife of the Prince of Wales and relying on the common abbreviation of the car-maker's name to 'Rolls'.

* **Cockroach** – *coach*. Evoking images of a decrepit old vehicle on a mystery tour.

* **Crowded space** – *suitcase*. A rhyme believed to be derived from the thieves' habit of lifting suitcases from busy stations.

* **Davey Large** – *barge*. After a nineteenth-century docker and a prominent trade unionist.

* **Frog in the throat** – *boat*. Going in a *frog* makes having a ride on the *fisherman's daughter* (*water*) a rather more innocent enterprise than it might at first sound.

* **Gay Gordon** – *traffic warden*. Possibly an innocent nod to the traditional ceilidh dance but more likely a non-PC pun suggesting assumptions about the sexuality of these unpopular professionals.

* **Grey mare** – *fare*. From the days when one was more likely to get a horse-drawn hansom cab than a bus.

* **Halfpenny dip** – *ship*. The rhyme alludes to making your choice in a sweetshop by having a lucky dip in a jar and dates from the nineteenth century, no doubt birthed in the docks where huge vessels were a constant presence.

* **Horse and carriage** – *garage*. A quirky rhyme referencing a mode of transport that the garage has played a vital role in supplanting.

* **Jam jar** – *car*. This rhyme is now used as the name of a popular website dedicated to the sale of second-hand motor vehicles. Not to be confused with ...

* ... **Jar of jam** – *tram*.

* **Jellied eels** – *wheels*.

* **Joe Baxi** – *taxi*. After an American heavyweight boxer briefly famous in post-war Britain for a fight against the then British champion, Bruce Woodcock.

Black Cabs

If you want to hear some genuine London slang, you could do worse than get in the back of a black cab. If you are lucky, you will get to hear some of the city's most authentic talk.

London's black cabs are all licensed, following a tradition established in 1662 when the government decided to regulate the business of the horse-drawn 'hackney carriages' that were for hire to the public. The last of these came off the capital's streets in 1947. Today there are some 21,000 automotive black cabs, with every driver required to pass the Knowledge test, an exacting examination of their grasp of the city's geography. A central London cabbie must know 320 routes (including landmarks and places of interest) within a six-mile radius of Charing Cross.

---

* **Pat and Mike** – *bike*. A Victorian rhyme that conjures up two caricatured Irish navvies.

146

* **Pop goes the weasel** – *diesel*. Recalling the old nursery rhyme. There is a theory that the 'weasel' is rhyming slang for 'coat' (see p. 96), while 'pop' is slang for 'to pawn'. Such a reading does seem to fit the lyrics: 'Half a pound of tuppenny rice, / Half a pound of treacle. / That's the way the money goes, / Pop goes the weasel' - an exceedingly prescient observation on the price of diesel!

* **Pot and pan** – *van*. Also used is *Peter Pan*, after the 1904 play by J.M. Barrie about the little boy who never grew up.

* **Ruin and spoil** – *oil*. Another rhyme that now seems prescient, given our modern understanding of the polluting effects of this fuel.

* **Smash and grab** – *cab*. Bringing to mind notions of robbery that anyone who has had to pay a particularly steep fare can empathize with.

* **Trouble and fuss** – *bus*. A phrase alluding to the hassle sometimes involved in this mode of transport.

* **Westminster Abbey** – *cabbie*. A convenient rhyme based on one of London's most popular tourist (and thus cabbie) destinations.

SLANG IN ACTION

Bernard liked to go into town but found the *ball* too long because his *plates* weren't what they used to be. On this particular day he went up to the main road as usual and waited half an hour for the bendy *trouble*, which was late as usual. Bernard had a go at the driver then realized he didn't have the *grey* for a *bat*. So the driver threw him off, telling him 'On yer *pat*!'

Translation

Bernard liked to go into town but found the *walk* too long because his *feet* weren't what they used to be. On this particular day he went up to the main road as usual and waited half an hour for the bendy *bus*, which was late as usual. Bernard had a go at the driver then realized he didn't have the *fare* for a *ticket*. So the driver threw him off, telling him 'On yer *bike*!'

—⚮—

Adam and Eve – *believe*. Another of those bits of rhyming slang that the whole world understands. People from all walks of life may occasionally be heard to say (usually slightly despairingly), 'I don't Adam and Eve it!' Adam and Eve were, of course, the first humans according to the Bible.

—⚏—

While a great deal of rhyming slang is, as you have seen, devoted to crime, dodgy dealings, sex and crudity, it is good to see that there is a (albeit small) spiritual element too!

* **Bag of yeast** – *priest*. A not overly flattering rhyme for men of the cloth.

* **Brown bread** – *dead*. A rhyme only in wide circulation for some forty years, but successor to older *bread* rhymes. Continues the association between bread and life.

* **Fork and knife** – *life*. A Victorian rhyme that acknowledges the fundamental importance of eating. Also *trouble and strife*, used less commonly than for *wife*, but emphasizing the difficulties incumbent in existence.

149

* **Hers and hims** – *hymns*. An obvious pun.

* **Lean and lurch** – *church*. A rather cutting rhyme given the poor physical condition of many old churches in the UK. Also used is *left in the lurch*, painting a picture of a lone figure at the altar and a wedding day gone wrong.

* **Overcoat maker** – *undertaker*. A dark rhyme playing on the slang term *wooden overcoat* for a coffin.

* **Peas and rice** – *Jesus Christ*. A relatively recent addition to the lexicon. Peas and rice is a dish synonymous with the Caribbean (the peas actually being beans).

* **Pie and liquor** – *vicar*. Liquor here is gravy and represents one of the staple foods of the old East End – the staff of life as it were. An alternative rhyme is *half a nicker* (equivalent to 10/-), perhaps alluding to the collection box circulated at religious services.

* **Pillar and post** – *ghost* (particularly the Holy Ghost). Pillar and post is a phrase believed to be derived from the game of real tennis around the fourteenth century. It may also hark back to the days when criminals faced punishment via whipping posts and pillories, bringing to mind notions of sin and atonement. Alternatively, *piece of toast*.

Bow Bells

The famous Bow Bells so crucial to the Cockney identity (see box on p. 21) are to be found in the church of St Mary-le-Bow in Cheapside in the City of London, built in 1080. The clear, crisp peal of its bells served as a curfew bell at nine o'clock each night, a sign that the city gates should be closed. Legend has it that the bells persuaded the three-times Lord Mayor of London, Dick Whittington, not to leave the city in his youth, beseeching him: 'Turn again, Whittington, Lord Mayor of London.'

The building was destroyed in the Great Fire of London in 1666 but rebuilt in a grand Baroque style by Christopher Wren. Since then the bells have remained part of London folklore. The 'Great Bell of Bow' features in the children's song 'Oranges and Lemons', with one theory going that their sound heralded an imminent execution at nearby Newgate. On 10 May 1941 the church fell victim to the Blitz bombing and the bells reputedly crashed to the ground, not to sound again until 1961. Today there are twelve bells in the church, the largest of which weighs forty-one hundredweight.

* **Tommy Dodd** – *God*. Probably an adaption of the rhyme *Tommy Dodds* for *odds*, perhaps reflecting a sense that life is beyond the control of mere mortals.

SLANG IN ACTION

When I was just a kid, starting out on the long road of *fork*, I felt a calling to be a *bag of yeast*. I attended church diligently three times a week (twice on Sundays) and was well known for singing my *strawberry* out during the *hers*. But then my faith was broken. I was due to have a chat with our respected *pie* but he never appeared. Turned out he'd run off with the organist's wife and the collection money they'd saved for the roof. No, I couldn't *adam* it either.

Translation

When I was just a kid, starting out on the long road of *life*, I felt a calling to be a *priest*. I attended church diligently three times a week (twice on Sundays) and was well known for singing my *heart* out during the *hymns*. But then my faith was broken. I was due to have a chat with our respected *vicar* but he never appeared. Turned out he'd run off with the organist's wife and the collection money they'd saved for the roof. No, I couldn't *believe* it either.

—⁘—

ENGLISH TO SLANG INDEX

Ace Cat's face
Arm Chalk Farm
Army Daft and barmy
Arse Aristotle (arris), Bottle and glass, Khyber Pass, Myleene Klass
Arsehole Elephant and Castle
Baby Basin of gravy
Back Haystack, Penny black
Bad Jack the Lad, Sorry and sad
Bail Royal Mail
Baked beans Kings and queens
Bald Cyril Lord
Balls Cobblers' awls, Henry Halls, Max Walls, Orchestra stalls
Bank Iron tank
Bar Jack tar
Barge Davey Large
Barmy Dad's Army, Salvation Army
Barrow Cock sparrow
Basin Charley Mason
Bath Hat and scarf
Beak Bubble and squeak
Beans Kings and queens
Beard Just as I feared
Beaver Sigourney Weaver
Bed Uncle Ned
Beef Itchy teeth
Beer Christmas cheer
Beers Britney Spears

Begger Peg-legger
Belch Raquel Welch
Believe Adam and Eve
Bell Little Nell
Belly Darby Kelly
Bent Bottle of scent
Bet National Debt
Big Smoke (London) Old Oak
Big Porky pig
Bike Pat and Mike
Bill Rhubarb pill
Bingo George and Ringo
Bins Errol Flynns
Bird Richard the Third
Bitch Miss Fitch
Bitter Giggle and titter
Black Coalman's sack, Jumping jack
Blade First aid, Shovel and spade
Blind Bacon rind
Blister Ugly Sister
Bloke Bushel of coke
Blow Rotten Row
Blower Percy Thrower
Blue Danny la Rue
Boat Frog in the throat
Body Big Ears and Noddy
Bog Cat and dog
Bogie Jimmy Logie
Boil Conan Doyle
Bollocks Sandra Bullocks
Bones Sticks and stones

153

Bonkers Marbles and conkers
Book Captain Cook, Rookery Nook
Bookie Cream cookie
Boots Daisy roots
Booze Mud and ooze, Pick and choose, River Ouse
Borrow Tomorrow
Boss Dead loss
Bottle Aristotle
Bouncer Half-ouncer
Boy Scout Brussels sprout
Boy Pride and joy, Rob Roy, Saveloy
Bra Ooh-la-la
Braces Epsom races
Brain Watch and chain
Brandy Amos and Andy, Fine and dandy
Brat Jack Sprat
Bread Needle and thread
Break Charlie Drake
Breasts Cabman's rests
Breath Life and death
Bride Fat and wide, Mother's pride
Broke Coal and coke
Broom Bride and groom
Brother Manhole cover
Brown Half a crown
Brussels sprouts Cockles and mussels
Bucket Mrs Ducket
Bum Big bass drum
Bunion Spanish onion
Burp Wyatt Earp
Bus Trouble and fuss
Butter Calcutta, Cough and splutter
Button Leg of mutton, Len Hutton
Cab Smash and grab
Cabbie Westminster Abbey
Candle Harry Randall
Car Jam jar
Cards Coldstream Guards

Carrots Polly parrots
Cash Bangers and mash
Cat Ball of fat
Ceiling Funny feeling
Cell Flowery dell
Chair Trafalgar Square, Vanity Fair
Chalk Lambeth Walk
Chance Charles Dance
Charlie Boutros Boutros-Ghali
Cheat Daisy beat
Cheque Goose's neck
Chest East and West, Mae West
Chicken Charlie Dicken
Chill Frock and frill
Chilly Uncle Willie
Chin Gunga Din
Chopper Gobstopper
Chump Lump and bump
Church Lean and lurch, Left in the lurch
Cider Runner and rider
Cigar La-di-dah
Cinders Polly Flinders
Clap (the) Horse and trap
Claret Eighteen carat
Cleaner Semolina
Clever Now and never
Clock Dickory-dock, Postman's Knock
Clown Charlie Brown
Club Rub-a-dub-dub
Clue Scooby-doo
Coach Cockroach
Coal Merry old soul
Coat Pound note, Quaker oat, Weasel and stoat
Cock Grandfather clock, Blackpool rock
Cocoa Orinoko
Cod Richard Todd
Coffee Everton toffee
Cold Naughton and Gold, Potatoes in the mould, Soldiers bold
Collar and tie Swallow and sigh

Condom Reggie and Ronnie
Copper Bottle and stopper
Cords House of Lords
Corns Cape Horns
Cough Horse and trough
Cousin Baker's dozen
Cow Ruck and row
Cowards Frankie Howerds
Crabs Beattie and Babs
Cramp Rising damp
Crap Andy Capp, Pony and trap
Creep Uriah Heep
Crook Babbling brook
Crutch Lord Sutch
Cry Pipe your eye
Cuddle Mix and muddle
Cunt Berkeley Hunt, James Blunt,
    Sir Anthony Blunt, Eyes front,
    Growl and grunt
Cup Dog and pup
Curry Ruby Murray
Curtain Richard Burton
Dance Kick and prance, South of
    France
Darts Horses and Carts
Daughter Bottle of porter, Soap
    and water
Day Blue and grey
Dead Brown bread
Deaf Mutt and Jeff
Diamond Simple Simon
Dice Rats and mice
Diesel Pop goes the weasel
Diet Brixton riot
Digs Ronnie Biggs
Dinner Lilley & Skinner
Dock Brighton Rock
Dog Cherry Hog, London fog
Dole (the) Sausage roll
Door Rory O'More
Double Rasher and bubble
Dress More or less
Drill Benny Hill
Drink Tiddlywink
Dripping Dr Crippen
Drunk Elephant's trunk

Dyke Raleigh bike
Ears Bottle of beers
Easy Bright and breezy
Eels Tommy Steeles
Egg Borrow and beg
Eight Garden gate
Erection General election
Eyes Mince pies
Face Boat race, Chevy Chase,
    Glass case, Jem Mace
Facts Brass tacks
Fag Cough and drag
Fake Cornflake
Fare Grey mare
Fart D'Oyly Carte, Raspberry tart
Father Soap and lather
Feet Dog's meat, Plates of meat
Fence Eighteen pence
Fiddle Hey-diddle-diddle
Fifty Nifty
Fight Dynamite, Read and write
Fighter Typewriter
Fine Bottle of wine
Finger Long and linger
Fingernails Worms and snails
Fire Aunt Maria, Black Maria
Firearms Fire alarms
First Geoff Hurst
Fish Lillian Gish
Fist Oliver Twist
Five Beehive
Fiver Lady Godiva
Flairs Lionel Blairs
Fleas Stand at ease
Floor Rory O'More
Flowers April showers
Flu Inky blue
Flutter Grumble and mutter
Fly Meat pie
Flying Squad Sweeney Todd
Food In the mood, In the nude
Fool Sharper's tool
Football pools April fools
Foreman Joe O'Gorman
Fork Duke of York, Roast pork,
    Joe Rourke

Four Knock on the door
Freezer Julius Caesar, Mona Lisa
French tricks Flying sixty-six
Fridge London Bridge
Friend Mile End
Fuck Aylesbury duck, Trolley and truck
Fucker Pheasant plucker
Gal Pall Mall
Gam Plate of ham
Garage Horse and carriage
Garden Beg your pardon, Dolly Varden
Gash Leslie Ash
Gay C&A, Doris Day
Geezer Lemon squeezer
Ghost Pillar and post
Gin Mother's ruin, Vera Lynn
Girl Ivory pearl, Twist and curl, Mother of pearl, Ribbon and curl
Glasses Mountain passes
Gloves Turtle doves
Go Scapa Flow
God Tommy Dodd
Good Robin Hood
Grand Bag of sand
Grass Old iron and brass
Gravy Army and Navy
Grey Night and day
Ground Safe and sound
Gun Hot cross bun
Gut Limehouse Cut
Guts Newington Butts
Gutter Bread and butter
Haddock Bessie Braddock
Haemorrhoids Emma Freuds
Hair Alf Garnett, Barnet Fair
Ham Trolley and tram
Hammer Stutter and stammer
Hand German band, Margate Sands
Handle Harry Randle
Hanky Widow Twankey
Hat Tit-for-tat
Head Loaf of bread

Heart Strawberry tart
Hearts Jam tarts
Hill Jack and Jill
Holy Ghost Piece of toast
Home Gates of Rome
Hooter Peashooter
Hoover Vancouver
Horn Flake of corn
Horse Charing Cross
Hot Peas in the pot
House Cat and mouse
Hymns Hers and hims
Ice Sugar and spice
Itch Little Tich
Jacket Fag packet
Jacksie London taxi
Jail Bucket and pale
Jaw Jackdaw
Jeans Baked beans
Jesus Christ Peas and rice
Jewellery Tomfoolery
Job Couple of bob
Judge Barnaby Rudge
Kettle Hansel and Gretel
Key Knobbly knee
Kid Gawd forbid, Saucepan lid
King Gold ring
Kip Feather and flip
Kipper Jack the Ripper
Kiss Hit and miss
Knackered Cream-crackered
Knackers Jacob's Cream Crackers
Knees Birds and bees, Biscuits and cheese
Knickers Alan Whickers, Brenda Frickers
Knife Drum and fife, Man and wife
Knob Uncle Bob
Labour exchange Beggar-my-neighbour
Ladder Leaky bladder
Ladies (toilets) Rosie O'Grady's
Lamb Uncle Sam
Lark Bushey Park
Late Harry Tate

Later Alligator
Laugh Bubble bath, Cow and calf, Steffi Graf
Lazy Gert and Daisy
Leak Zorba the Greek
Legs Clothes pegs, Scotch pegs
Liar Dunlop tyre, Holy friar
Lick Pat and Mick
Lie Pork pie
Life Fork and knife, Trouble and strife
Lips Apple pips, Battleships
Live Take and give
Liver Bow and quiver
Lodger Artful Dodger, Jolly Roger
Look Butcher's hook
Loon Keith Moon, Man in the Moon
Loot Whistle and toot
Lug Toby jug
Mad Mum and Dad
Magistrate Garden gate
Man Pot and pan
Market pitch Hedge and ditch
Match Colney Hatch
Matches Cuts and scratches
Mate China plate
Meat Hands and feet
Mental Radio rental
Milk Yellow silk
Minute Cock linnet
Missus Cow and kisses
Moke Jerusalem artichoke
Money Bread and honey
Moody Punch and Judy
Moon Silver spoon
Morning Gypsy's warning, Maids adorning
Mother God love her, Strangle and smother
Mouse Maxwell House
Moustache Whip and lash
Mouth North and South
Mrs Chant's (lavatory) My aunt's
Mug Barge and tug, Steam tug
Muscles Greens and Brussels

Mussels Jane Russells
Mutton Billy Button
Nail Monkey's tail
Nancy Tickle your fancy
Nark Noah's Ark
Nerves West Ham Reserves
Newspaper Linen draper, Skyscraper
Nice Apples and rice
Nick Shovel and pick
Night Black and white
Nine Mother of mine
Nipples Raspberry ripples
Noise Girls and boys
Nose Ruby rose
Nutter Brandy butter
Odds Tommy Dodds
Oil Ruin and spoil
Old Bill Beecham's pill
Old girl Mother of pearl
Old man Old pot and pan
On your own On your Darby and Joan, Jack Jones, Tod Sloan
On your way! Edna May
One Penny bun
Onions Corns and bunions
Organ Captain Morgan
Paddock Smoked haddock
Pain Hangar Lane, Petticoat Lane
Pants Fleas and ants
Park Joan of Arc
Parole Jam roll
Party Hail and hearty
Peas Yous and mes
Peck Tooting Bec
Pee Cup of tea
Pen Bill and Ben
Penis Mars and Venus
Penny Abergavenny
Pension Stand to attention
Pepper High stepper
Piano Joanna
Pickle Slap and tickle
Pictures (the) Fleas and itches
Piddle Jimmy Riddle
Pig Lord Wigg

Pig's trotters Gillie Potters
Piles Annabel Giles, Chalfont St Giles, Johnny Giles
Pillow Weeping willow
Pills Jack and Jills, Fanny Hills
Pinch half-inch
Pink Rinky dink
Pipe Cherry ripe
Piss Cuddle and kiss, Gypsy's kiss, Snake's hiss
Pissed Brahms and Lizst
Pisshole Savoury rissole
Pistol Lady from Bristol
Plants Uncles and aunts
Plate Harry Tate
Play Night and day
Plug Little brown jug
Pocket Lucy Locket
Ponce Alphonse
Pong Anna May Wong
Pony Macaroni
Poof Iron hoof
Poor On the floor
Pork Duchess of York
Port Didn't ought
Post Tea and toast
Pot Sir Walter Scott
Potato Navigator
Pound Lost and found
Pout Salmon and trout
Pox East India Docks, Tilbury Docks
Pratt Top hat
Prawn Frankie Vaughan
Prick Hampton Wick, Lionel Hampton
Priest Bag of yeast
Pub Rub-a-dub
Puff Nellie Duff
Pull John Bull
Punter Billy Bunter
Queen Baked bean, Mary Green
Queer Brighton Pier, Ginger beer
Race course Iron horse
Races Belt and braces
Rain France and Spain

Randy Port and brandy
Rat Bowler hat
Razor House of Fraser
Readies Nelson Eddies
Red Bald head
Rent Burton on Trent, Duke of Kent
Right Harbour light
River Bullock's liver
Road Frog and Toad
Rolls-Royce Camilla Parker Bowles
Room Shovel and broom
Rotten Billy Cotton
Row Bull and cow
Rum Finger and thumb
Runs (the) Radio Ones, Tommy guns
Sack (the) Last card of the pack
Sack Roberta Flack
Salt Squad halt
Sandals Roman candles
Saucer Geoffrey Chaucer
Sausages Bags of mystery
Saw Mother-in-law
Scarf Half and half
Score Charlie Clore
Scotland Yard Bladder of lard
Screw Little Boy Blue, Me and you
Sea Coffee and tea
Sense Shillings and pence
Seven God in heaven
Sex Oedipus Rex, T Rex
Shag Melvyn Bragg
Shakes Currant cakes
Shandy Andy Pandy
Shares Rupert Bears
Shave Chas and Dave, Ocean wave
Sheep Bo Peep
Sherry Woolwich Ferry
Shiner Morris Minor, Ocean liner
Ship Halfpenny dip
Shirker Office worker
Shirt Dicky dirt

Shirty Uncle Bertie
Shit Tomtit
Shits (the) Eartha Kitts
Shitter Gary Glitter
Shoes Canoes, Jimmy Choos
Shooter Phil the Fluter
Shop Mrs Mopp
Shoulder Rock and boulder
Shovel Lord Lovell
Shower Eiffel Tower
Shrimp Colonel Blimp
Sick Tom and Dick
Silly Piccadilly
Sing Mangle and wring
Sister Skin and blister
Six Chopsticks
Skin Vera Lynn
Skint Boracic lint
Skive Duck and dive
Skiver Backseat driver
Sky Shepherd's pie
Slash Johnny Cash
Sleep Bo Peep
Slippers Pair of kippers
Smack Uncle Mac
Smell Heaven and hell, William Tell
Smile Crocodile
Smoke Laugh and joke
Sneeze Bread and cheese
Snide Mr Hyde
Snore Lion's roar, Rain and pour
Snow Duck and doe
Snuff Blind man's buff
Soap Bob Hope
Socks Almond rocks
Sod Haddock and cod
Son Currant bun
Song Ding-dong
Soup Bowl the Hoop
Spades Lemonade, Lucozades
Spanner Elsie Tanner
Sparrow Bow and arrow
Speed Lou Reed
Spider Sit beside her
Spinach Woolwich and Greenwich

Splinter Harold Pinter
Spoon Lorna Doone
Spots Randolph Scotts
Spunk Maria Monk, Thelonius Monk
Squirrel Nice one, Cyril
Stairs Apples and pears
Starting/winning post Holy Ghost
Starving Lee Marvin
State Two and eight
Steak and kidney Kate and Sidney
Steak Joe Blake
Stench Judi Dench
Stew Waterloo
Stink Pen and ink
Stockings Reelings and rockings
Story Jackanory
Stranger Queens Park Ranger
Street Field of wheat
Stripper Herring and kipper
Style Tate and Lyle
Suit Whistle and flute
Suitcase Crowded space
Sun Bath bun
Supper Tommy Tupper
Swear Rip and tear
Sweetheart Jam tart
Syphilis Lover's tiff
Table Cain and Abel
Tadger Fox and badger
Tail Brass nail
Tale Daily Mail, Newgate Gaol, Weep and wail
Talk Rabbit and pork
Talker Johnnie Walker
Tax Beeswax
Taxi Joe Baxi
Tea Rosie Lee
Teeth Hampstead Heath
Telephone Dog and bone, Trombone
Telly Mother Kelly, Roger Mellie
Ten Big Ben
Tenner Ayrton Senna
Thick King Dick
Thief Tea leaf

Thin Needle and pin
Third Douglas Hurd
Throat Nanny Goat
Throne Rag and bone
Thrush Basil Brush
Thumb Jamaica Rum
Thunder Stand from under
Ticket Bat and wicket
Tie Peckham Rye
Tights Fly-by-nights
Time Birdlime, Harry Lime
Tip Sherbert dip
Tits Brad Pitts, Eartha Kitts, Threepenny bits
Titties Bristol Cities
Toast Holy Ghost
Toes Seb Coes
Tonic Philharmonic
Tools Crown jewels, April fools
Tooth General Booth
Tote (the) Nanny goat
Towel Enoch Powell
Town Mother Brown
Traffic warden Gay Gordon
Trainers Claire Rayners, Struggle-and-strainers
Tram Jar of jam
Tramp Halfpenny stamp
Trey Vicar of Bray
Trouble Barney Rubble
Trousers Round the houses (Round the's)
Trowel Baden-Powell
Truth Maud and Ruth
Tune Stewed prune
Turd George the Third, Lemon curd, Richard the Third
Turkey Bubbly jock
Twat (twot) Glue pot
Twenty Horn of plenty
Twenty-four Pompey whore
Twig Earwig
Two Me and you
Two-one Attila the Hun
Two-two Desmond
Tyre Billy Liar

Umbrella Aunt Ella
Undertaker Overcoat maker
Undies Eddie Grundies
Van Pot and pan
Veg Uncle Reg
Vicar Half a nicker
Vicar Pie and liquor
Villain Harold Macmillan
Vino Quentin Tarantino
Violin Hey-diddle-diddle
Voice Hobson's Choice
Vomit Wallace and Gromit
Wages Greengages
Waistcoat Charlie Prescot, John Prescott
Waiter Hot potato
Walk Ball of chalk
Wank Barclays Bank, J. Arthur Rank, Sherman tank
Wanker Crown and anchor, Merchant banker
Warder Harry Lauder
Watch Gordon and Gotch
Water Fisherman's daughter
Weather Hat and feather
Weed Ollie Reed
Week Bubble and squeak
West Jacket and vest
Wheels Jellied eels
Whisky Bright and frisky
Whore Bolt the door, Jane Shore
Wife Duchess of Fife (Dutch), Light of my life, Trouble and strife
Wig Syrup of figs
Win Nose and chin
Wind Jenny Lind
Window Tommy Trinder
Windy Rawalpindi
Wine Plinkety plonk
Winkles Granny's wrinkles
Winner Hot dinner
Word Dicky bird
Work Smile and smirk
Wrong Pete Tong
Yellow Cinderella